Spiritual Leadership

Responding to God's Call

J. Oswald Sanders

with contributions by Neil Knierim and Yvonne Burrage

Original *Spiritual Leadership* text © 1967, 1980, 1994 by The Moody Bible Institute of Chicago
ISBN 0-8024-6799-7

Introduction and Interactive Activities © Copyright 1999 • LifeWay Press
ISBN 0-7673-9449-6

Dewey Decimal Classification: 253.2
Subject Heading:
MINISTERS / VOCATIONAL GUIDANCE / LEADERSHIP

Printed in the United States of America.

Pastor-Staff Leadership Department
LifeWay Christian Resources
of the Southern Baptist Convention
127 Ninth Avenue, North
Nashville, Tennessee 37234

Contents

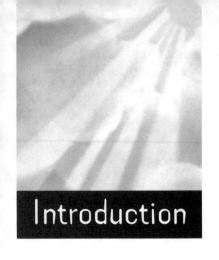

Introduction

The book, *Spiritual Leadership*, by J. Oswald Sanders is a classic. Many well-known Christian leaders have credited this book with making a tremendous impact on their lives and ministries. The first time I read this book was when I was serving as a youth minister while attending seminary. I was preparing to lead a group of adults through an extended training program to serve as small-group leaders in a youth discipleship strategy. *Spiritual Leadership* was one of the books required for each adult to study in preparation for the training course.

My first attempt at reading the book was overwhelming. For one starting out in the ministry, it was very challenging. I never before had considered that to be an effective church leader I would need to be a spiritual leader. The principles Sanders identified and explained were so challenging that I had to put the book down. They made demands on my life that I was not ready to deal with. I was just going to be a church leader. Several weeks passed before I was ready to read the book and let it impact my life.

The impact *Spiritual Leadership* makes on a person's life is why I want to provide the book in this new format. I am grateful to Moody Press for allowing Yvonne Burrage and me to present the classic truths in the book in a new way. Our hope is that it will impact your life as it has so many others.

Spiritual Leadership is helpful for any Christian who would like to grow in Christ and become more like Him; however, it is intended for persons who have sensed a call to vocational ministry. It also is intended to be a follow-up to the first book in the Calling Out the Called Series, *God's Call: The Cornerstone of Effective Ministry*.

God's Call is designed to help you know whether God is calling you into the ministry. It is essential for you to know God has called you if you are considering vocational ministry. *God's Call* examines several persons' call to the ministry to help you determine if God is calling you. It provides interactive activities to help you personalize information provided in the book. If you have not read and worked through *God's Call*, please consider purchasing a copy and working through it before you read and work through this book. It will help you to know for sure that God has called you into the ministry before you complete this study.

Why is it important for you to know that God has called you into the ministry? God calls every Christian to ministry. The Bible clearly teaches that once you have recognized that you are a sinner, repented from your sins, invited Christ into your heart, and committed your life to Him, then God comes into your life and heart. Once you have experienced Christ as your Savior, He wants to become the Lord of your life. As a part of His lordship, we serve Him through serving others. We follow the example Jesus set for us as recorded in the four Gospels—Matthew, Mark, Luke, and John. There we see that He not only shared the good news with people, but He also ministered to them by meeting their needs. Some of the needs were physical, others emotional; but all of Jesus' ministry actions were aimed at meeting people's spiritual needs. Every Christian is to follow His example. However, not all Christians are called to *the* ministry.

Vocational Ministry—God's Purpose and Plan for Me?

As every Christian grows in his or her Christian walk, God reveals to that person His plan for his or her life. Again, the Bible clearly points out that God has a purpose and plan for every person's life. God wants every person to be saved and to love Him with all his or her heart, mind, and soul. He also wants us to love one another. The Great Commandment and the Great Commission go together—to love God with all of our heart, to love one another as we do ourselves, and to tell others about Christ because we love them. These are general purposes for every person's life. But, God also has a specific plan for each individual. He has a plan for you. He has gifted you with spiritual gifts, given you special talents and abilities, and created your unique personality.

Discovering what God wants you to do with your life is a pursuit worth the effort. Just as He called persons to be leaders in biblical days, He still calls persons today to build His church through vocational ministry. If God has called you to the ministry, you must be ready to respond. It doesn't make you better than anyone else or more important, but it does magnify your responsibility. Imagine that the great God of the Universe has chosen you for the awesome responsibility and opportunity of leading His people. People who are not called should not be in *the* ministry; but, people who are called to *the* ministry will have a difficult time finding fulfillment in doing anything else. People go into vocational ministry for a variety of reasons. The only valid reason is that you have sensed and strongly believe God has called you into *the* ministry. Ministry is not a profession we choose but one that God calls us into. The book *God's Call* can help you determine if God is calling you.

Called into the Ministry—What Next?

Okay, so you feel strongly that God has called you into the ministry and you have committed your life to Him and will be a vocational minister. You ask, What do I do now? That is a great question. For some people it will be a number of years between committing themselves to vocational ministry and actually serving in some ministry capacity. For others it could be a few months. "What do I do now?" Don't worry about what type of ministry you will be doing. You may not know for a while.

The key isn't what you are going to do; the key is that you have committed your life to God, so whatever He leads you to do is going to be okay. As you wait for His direction, prepare yourself to be ready when God reveals His specific plan for you.

Seek the counsel of others.—It is important to talk with someone concerning your call to the ministry. Talk with your parents, your youth minister, your pastor, or someone you respect because of his or her spiritual insights and counsel. Oftentimes when you speak with others about sensing a call to the ministry, they will tell you that they already knew God was calling you. Sometimes others are aware of God's call on your life before you are. It is affirming when this happens. These persons can help you as you determine whether God is calling you into the ministry. They can advise you, pray with you, and pray for you. This is too important to sort through by yourself. Don't worry that

General calls

you might not be called into the ministry and then later be embarrassed. Those whom you talk with will be proud that you took the possibility of God's call on your life seriously. They will not think less of you if you determine that you were not called to the ministry. Their goal will be to help you discover God's plan.

I talked several times with a young man in our church who was graduating from high school. He is a fine young man who wants to do what God has planned for him. Because he is serious about his relationship with Christ, he felt that he might be experiencing a call to the ministry. He was very open about it with several of us in the congregation. He was trying to select a college to attend, and if he were to be a minister, that would impact his college selection. He and I talked a couple of times, and he also talked with others. At the present time he feels that he wants to serve God with his life but he doesn't feel that God is calling him to vocational ministry. His journey was significant. He has answered the question concerning ministry and now is pursuing other options. None of us felt it was wasted time to talk with him. It was beneficial to him to close this door and look to some other opportunities.

As you grow in your walk with the Lord, it may become clear that you are not called to the ministry, Again, it would be wise to discuss this with someone you respect and trust and who can offer you wise counsel. You don't need to feel embarrassed; it is great that you have the courage to deal with it and make the right decision.

Talk with your pastor and ask him for the opportunity to speak to the congregation. Thank them for their support and simply let them know that it has become clear to you that you are not called to the ministry and you now are considering other options for your life. They should be proud of you for sharing this development with them. It is a courageous act.

Make your commitment public.—Once you know for sure God has called you into the ministry, talk with your pastor. Under his counsel, when you are ready, let your church family know you are accepting God's call to the ministry. Your pastor will help you know how this is done in your church. Generally, during the invitation time of the Sunday morning or evening service you would go forward and inform the church of your decision. It should be a time of affirmation and celebration. It is also a serious time. The church now has a responsibility to help you prepare for the ministry. This is done by encouraging you, praying for you, teaching you, and providing opportunities to permit you to learn how to lead, preach, and minister. It also is an opportunity for you to make your commitment to vocational ministry public. In doing this, you are confirming for yourself that this is what God wants you to do. It no longer is a private matter; but because you are sure, you have made it known to every-one. This also builds accountability on your part. People will view you as one preparing for ministry, and their expectations for you will be higher.

How/Where Will I Serve?

Don't get frustrated or discouraged if you don't know for sure what type of ministry God is calling you into. Some people know they are to be a missionary to a particular country doing a certain thing. Others don't have any idea what God wants them to do but are willing to do whatever He asks. It may take time for you to discover your ministry role. And even then, it may change as you gain ministry experience. Don't make the mistake of feeling that God may not have called you because you don't know exactly what you are to do. Be faithful. Trust God. He will let you know in plenty of time.

When I made my commitment to vocational ministry I assumed I would be a preacher, a pastor. Since I committed my life to vocational ministry I have been a minister of children and youth, a minister of youth, a minister of education and administration, a pastor, a state convention worker, a pastor again, and a Sunday School Board/LifeWay Christian Resources worker. And I may be several other things before my ministry winds down. As mentioned earlier, what you are going to do is not as important as who you are going to become. God wants those He has called to be persons He can use, persons of character, and persons involved in the life of His church.

Am I a Person God Can Use?

Regardless of what you do in ministry, you will need to be a person God can use. Now is the time for you to become a strong, committed follower of Christ. To be a person who is growing into the image of Christ. One who is walking close to God, growing deeper and deeper in love with Him. This is what is important in every minister's life. Here are some things you can do:

• ***Develop a quiet time alone with God.***—Spend time reading the Scripture. Listen to what God is saying to you about who you are and about the quality of your life. Spend time praying for others and yourself. Invite God to work in your life. Develop a spiritual character. Bring your life under the lordship of Christ by confessing your sins to Him and asking for forgiveness. Ask God to reveal your sins to you. Thank Him for all He has given to you and your family. Thank Him for His presence in your life. Pray for the needs of your family, friends, and church family. Be in awe when you see those prayers answered.

• ***Read the Bible all the way through.***—Find a systematic approach to reading the Bible through in one year. As one who will be a minister, you need to develop an understanding of and a love for the Scriptures. The Bible tells us how we are to live. It provides examples for us to follow. The Bible teaches us about persons who faced tough challenges but were able to see God provide a way. It will help us in our daily living and our ministry if we permeate our minds with the Scripture.

• ***Study the Bible.***—Find a good Bible commentary and read and study the Bible. Read a passage of Scripture and ask the following questions: Who wrote this passage? When was it written? What was going on in the world when it was written? What is the main point of the passage? How does this apply to me today? Develop a notebook to store all of this information. Don't rush. Take your time.

• ***Memorize Scripture passages.***—Identify key passages and meditate on them. Commit them to memory. Ask God to help you recall these passages when you are tempted or need to be reminded of His power and grace.

Does My Life Honor Christ?

Another aspect of becoming a person whom God can use is developing a life of character. In First Timothy, Paul has some great words of instruction. A careful study of this letter will help you see how important it is for a minister to become a godly person. While every Christian is held to a high standard of conduct and living, ministers appear to have an even higher standard. This means that we must be diligent in following Christ's example. We must be careful to live in a way that honors Christ. Others know that you are committed to vocational ministry. They will watch what you do, listen to what you say, and expect more from you. Being faithful to God, being a good steward of what God entrusts to you, and being pure are ways to demonstrate to people that you are serious about your calling. Being honest, truthful, and respectful of others reflects your commitment to Christ. It builds good habits for the future.

Many ministers have disqualified themselves from the ministry because they have made a mistake. They got involved in an inappropriate sexual relationship, mishandled money or their own personal finances, or they were unethical in some way. It is important to tell the truth, not to cheat, and to do the right things. The Scriptures lift up the qualifications of the minister. Living right as you prepare for ministry will help you live right as a minister.

What Can I Do Now to Prepare for the Ministry?

Another important aspect of becoming a person God can use is to get involved in church activities. If you are a teenager, get involved in the youth activities in your church. If your church is small, participate in associational youth activities.

- *Attend Sunday School.*
- *Participate in the discipleship programs in your church.*—Take advantage of the opportunities to learn from your leaders and other teenagers.
- *Get involved in outside Bible studies like devotional times before school, small-group Bible studies, and other opportunities for Bible study.*
- *Participate in mission trips and other similar opportunities like Backyard Bible Clubs, and so on.*
- *Volunteer to lead devotions at youth events to gain some experience in leading groups in spiritual activities.*
- *Attend sessions to learn how to share your faith with others.*—Find someone in your church who is an effective soul winner and ask if you can go visiting with him or her to learn how to witness to others.
- *Participate in Royal Ambassadors or Acteens if your church offers these missions education programs.*—It will help you learn about missionaries and mission opportunities.
- *Volunteer to teach a Sunday School class at different times of the year.*—Ask to teach preschoolers, children, your own class, and an adult class. It will give you experience in teaching the Bible to others. Whatever ministry role you eventually pursue, you will need to be able to teach the Bible clearly and effectively.
- *Speak at a youth rally.*—Ask your youth minister or pastor to teach you how to prepare a sermon. Work with them as you develop the sermon so they

can give you some helpful hints along the way. If you prepare the sermon on your own, ask someone to look it over and offer suggestions.

- ***Ask the pastor or another staff member to take you visiting with them.***—Go to the hospital or call on a shut-in.
- ***Ask your pastor and/or other staff members to teach you about their duties.***—Ask them what they do, how they prepared for their role, and how you might be able to help. See if they will let you job shadow them from time to time. Learn from them.
- ***When guest preachers and leaders come to your church, ask the appropriate person if you can meet them and learn from them.***—Listen to them and learn from their experiences. If possible, ask them questions about their ministry and how they prepared for it.
- ***Ask if you can attend some of the committee meetings in your church to learn how committees operate and what their duties are.***— Whatever your ministry role will be, you will need to understand how the church operates and how committees function.
- ***Find places to lead worship services.***—If you feel led to the music ministry, lead music at nursing homes, hospitals, missions, shelters, jails, and so on. The same is true if you feel led to a preaching or teaching ministry. Look for places where you can learn by doing and gain experience.
- ***Work hard in school.***—Learn how to study. Make good grades in order to open doors at colleges and seminaries. Take English classes to develop your grammar skills. Take speech classes and participate in speech tournaments. This will help you feel comfortable while speaking in front of people and to groups. Consider participating on a debate team to develop research and thinking skills. Debaters have to develop the ability to think quickly. Enroll in a variety of writing classes. This will help you be able to put your thoughts in order. It will enhance your presentation skills and serve you well in sermon and teaching preparation. Develop a love for learning.
- ***Start thinking about colleges and seminaries.***—Begin to explore the colleges you would like to attend. Consider a Baptist college or other Christian schools. Look at their academics and spiritual atmosphere. If you will be attending a state school, learn all you can about the student ministry opportunities offered on the campus. Ask about churches that have ministries for college students. Begin exploring which seminary you might attend. Talk with seminary representatives and discover what you need to do academically in college to enter that particular seminary. Some colleges have special relationships with seminaries so that you can do a coordinated curriculum plan.
- ***Learn how to relate to people.***—Study them and develop an understanding of how people think and react. Much of your work in ministry is people centered. Make friends. Develop relationships with a variety of people. The ability to relate to people will have a major impact on your future ministry.
- ***Attend seminars and conferences for persons who are pursuing vocational ministry.***—More and more associations and state conventions are offering these conferences. It is encouraging to be with others who are experiencing the same things that you are.

- **_Enroll in the Vocational Guidance Directory._**—Use the form in the back of this book to enroll. Complete the form and send it to the address given on the form. It will put you in a database that will keep you informed of ministry, mission, and conference opportunities. The Vocational Guidance ministry of LifeWay Christian Resources will keep you informed of new resources and training opportunities just for persons pursuing vocational ministry. Encouragement and information are just two ways this ministry will assist you. You will have your name in a database with thousands of people who are seeking God's will for their life by pursuing vocational ministry.

- **_Work hard and have fun._**—Being in the ministry is not something to be sad about or to make you extremely serious. Enjoy life and become the person God wants you to be. You are unique. Celebrate your uniqueness and have fun.

If you are a college student or someone already established in a career who is sensing God's call to the ministry, look over this list. Many of the suggestions apply to you as well. There is no need to feel that you have to wait to be in a ministry position before you can prepare for and actively participate in ministry activities. Whether you are a high school, college, or career person who feels called to the ministry, you can find mentors to help you in your preparation and to serve as coaches/encouragers as you develop as a minister. Ask questions. Learn from these people.

Becoming a Spiritual Leader

Reading this book and working through the activities will help you personalize and apply the truths in this book. You are taking a huge first step in becoming a spiritual leader. Remember this: God is calling you to be a spiritual leader if He has called you to the ministry. The business world says a great deal about leadership and the importance of being a leader. You will find a number of books that describe how to become a leader. These books will be helpful, and the principles they share are good. But, there is a great difference between being an effective corporate leader and an effective spiritual leader. Earlier I mentioned that it was difficult for me to read this book for the first time over 20 years ago. I thought I was becoming a good church leader. I knew a lot about church organization, resources, process, training, and other procedural things. But I had not learned that God didn't call me to be a good manager, administrator, and so on. He called me—and I am confident He is calling you—to be a spiritual leader first and foremost.

Read this book. Work through the activities. Personalize the teachings and principles in this book. Take your time, and let the timeless truths that J. Oswald Sanders has shared with thousands of other ministers impact your life. Work through it over and over. The truths in this book are too valuable to read through just once. Return to it throughout your ministry.

May God bless your life and your ministry. May you find complete fulfillment in giving your life in service to Him and those He died for. Above everything else in your ministry, desire to know intimately the One who called you and that your ministry be empowered by Him. Be a leader in the kingdom. Be a spiritual leader.

An Honorable Ambition

To aspire to leadership is an honorable ambition. ✓
—1 Timothy 3:1, NEB

Should you then seek great things for yourself? Seek them not. ✓
—Jeremiah 45:5, NIV

Is it right to want to be a leader?

Most Christians have reservations about aspiring to leadership. They are unsure about whether it is truly right for a person to want to be a leader. After all, is it not better for the position to seek out the person rather than the person to seek out the position? Has not ambition caused the downfall of several otherwise great leaders in the church, people who fell victim to "the last infirmity of noble minds"? Shakespeare expressed a profound truth when his character Wolsey said to the great English general:

>   Cromwell, I charge thee, fling away ambitions,
>   By that sin fell the angels; how can a man then,
>   The image of his Maker, hope to profit by't?[1]

No doubt, Christians must resist a certain kind of ambition and rid it from their lives. But we also must acknowledge other ambitions as noble, worthy, and honorable. The two verses at the beginning of this chapter provide a warning and an encouragement for sorting out the difference.

Read 1 Timothy 3:1 (NEB). Describe your leadership ambition.

I need to be broken before God + use the abilities he has given me to lead or follow which ever He desires. I am willing!!

When our ambition is to be effective in the service of God—to realize God's highest potential for our lives—we can keep both of these verses in mind and hold them in tension.

Part of that tension is the difference between Paul's situation and ours. We may understand his statement in terms of the prestige and respect given to Christian leaders today. But such was far from Paul's mind. In his day, a bishop faced great danger and worrisome responsibility. Rewards for the work of leading the church were hardship, contempt, and rejection. The leader was the first to draw fire in persecution, the first in line to suffer.

Seen in this light, Paul's encouragement does not seem so open to misuse by people merely seeking status in the church. Phonies would have little heart for such a difficult assignment. Under the dangerous circumstances which prevailed in the first century, even stout-hearted Christians needed encouragement and incentive to lead. And so Paul called leadership an "honorable ambition."

The same situation faces Christians today in certain parts of the world. Leaders of the church in China suffered most at the hands of Communists. The pastor of the Little Flock in Nepal suffered years in prison after church members had been released. In many troubled areas today, spiritual leadership is no task for those who seek stable benefits and upscale working conditions.

Paul urges us to the work of leading the church, the most important work in the world. When our motives are right, this work pays eternal dividends. In Paul's day, only a deep love for Christ and genuine concern for the church could motivate people to lead. But in many cultures today where Christian leadership carries prestige and privilege, people aspire to leadership for reasons quite unworthy and self-seeking.

And so Jeremiah gave Baruch some wise and simple counsel: "Should you then seek great things for yourself? Seek them not" (Jer. 45:5). The prophet was not condemning all ambition as sinful, but he was pointing to selfish motivation that makes ambition wrong—"great things *for yourself*." Desiring to be great is not a sin. It is motivation that determines ambition's character. Our Lord never taught against the urge to high achievement, but He did expose and condemn unworthy motivation.

All Christians are called to develop God-given talents, to make the most of their lives, to develop to the fullest their God-given powers and capacities. But Jesus taught that ambition that centers on the self is wrong. Speaking to young ministers about to be ordained, the great missionary leader Bishop Stephen Neill said: "I am inclined to think that ambition in any ordinary sense of the term is nearly always sinful in ordinary men. I am certain that in the Christian it is always sinful, and that it is most inexcusable of all in the ordained minister."[2]

Ambition that centers on the glory of God and welfare of the church is a mighty force for good.

The word *ambition* comes from a Latin word meaning "campaigning for promotion." The phrase suggests a variety of elements: social visibility and approval, popularity, peer recognition, the exercise of authority over others. Ambitious people, in this sense, enjoy the power that comes with money and authority. Jesus had no time for such ego-driven ambitions. The true spiritual leader will never "campaign for promotion."

To His "ambitious" disciples Jesus announced a new standard of greatness: "You know that those who are regarded as rulers of the Gentiles lord it over them, and their high officials exercise authority over them. Not so with you. Instead, whoever wants to become great among you must be your servant, and whoever wants to be first must be slave of all" (Mark 10:42-44). We will consider this amazing statement in a later chapter.

At the outset of any study of spiritual leadership, this master principle must be squarely faced: True greatness, true leadership, is found in giving yourself in service to others, not in coaxing or inducing others to serve you. True service is never without cost. Often it comes with a painful baptism of suffering. But the true spiritual leader is focused on the service he and she can render to God and other people, not on the residuals and perks of high office or holy title. We must aim to put more into life than we take out.

A true spiritual leader focuses his life on . . .

Serving others not gaining self ambitions

"One of the outstanding ironies of history is the utter disregard of ranks and titles in the final judgments men pass on each other," said Samuel Brengle, the great Salvation Army revival preacher. "The final estimate of men shows that history cares not an iota for the rank or title a man has borne, or the office he has held, but only the quality of his deeds and the character of his mind and heart."[3]

Summarize in your own words the point that Samuel Brengle made regarding the heart of a spiritual leader.

The title is not what is important when looking at the effectiveness of a leader but the quality of what he has done and how he got that accomplished it.

"Let it once be fixed that a man's ambition is to fit into God's plan for him, and he has a North Star ever in sight to guide him steadily over any sea, however shoreless it seems," wrote S. D. Gordon in one of his well-known devotional books. "He has a compass that points true in the thickest fog and fiercest storm, and regardless of magnetic rocks."

The great leader Count Nikolaus von Zinzendorf (1700–1760) was tempted by rank and riches; indeed, he is most widely known by the title of honor noted here. But his attitude toward ambition was summed up in one simple statement: "I have one passion: it is He, He alone." Zinzendorf turned from self-seeking to become the founder and leader of the Moravian church. His followers learned from their leader and circled the world with his passion. Before missionary work was popular or well-organized, the Moravians established overseas churches which had three times as many members as did their churches back home—a most unusual accomplishment. Indeed, one of every 92 Moravians left home to serve as a missionary.

> Because we children of Adam want to become great,
> He became small.
> Because we will not stoop,
> He humbled Himself.
> Because we want to rule,
> He came to serve.

---

[1] Shakespeare, *Henry VIII,* Act 3, Scene 2.
[2] Stephen Neill, "Address to Ordinands," *The Record*, 28 March 1947, 161. Neill (1900–1984) served in South India and later taught missiology.
[2] C. W. Hall, *Samuel Logan Brengle* (New York: Salvation Army, 1933), 274. Brengle (1860–1939) was internationally sought as a holiness speaker during the early decades of this century.

The Search for Leaders

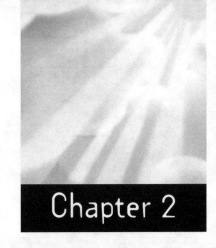

No one from the east or the west
  or from the desert can exalt a man.
But it is God who judges:
  He brings one down, he exalts another.
                        —Psalm 75:6-7

Give me a man of God—one man,
  One mighty prophet of the Lord,
And I will give you peace on earth,
  Bought with a prayer and not a sword.
                        —George Liddell[1]

Real leaders are in short supply. Constantly people and groups search for them. Throughout the Bible, God searches for leaders, too.

"The LORD has sought out a man after his own heart and appointed him leader of his people" (1 Sam. 13:14).

memory verse

"Go up and down the streets of Jerusalem, look around and consider, search through her squares. If you can find but one person who deals honestly and seeks the truth, I will forgive this city" (Jer. 5:1).

"I looked for a man among them who would build up the wall" (Ezek. 22:30).

Identify possible reasons for a short supply of church leaders today.

Those not seeking after God's own heart they are seeking their heart.

ego.
selfishness
material desires

i Sam 13:14

fear

want to be in the lime light

The Bible shows us that when God does find a person who is ready to lead, to commit to full discipleship and take on responsibility for others, that person is used to the limit. Such leaders still have shortcomings and flaws; but despite those, they become spiritual leaders. Such were Moses, Gideon, and David; and in the history of the church, Martin Luther, John Wesley, Adoniram Judson, William Carey, and many others.

To be a leader in the church has always required strength and faith beyond the merely human. Why is our need for leaders so great, yet candidates for leadership so few? Every generation faces the stringent demands of spiritual leadership and welcomes the few who come forward to serve.

"The church is painfully in need of leaders," lamented the English Methodist preacher William Sangster. "I wait to hear a voice and no voice comes. . . . I would rather listen than speak—but there is no clarion voice to listen to."[2]

If the world is to hear the church's voice today, leaders are needed who are authoritative, spiritual, and sacrificial. Authoritative, because people desire leaders who know where they are going and are confident of getting there. Spiritual, because without a strong relationship to God, even the most attractive and competent person cannot lead people to God. Sacrificial, because this follows the model of Jesus, who gave Himself for the whole world and who calls us to follow in His steps.

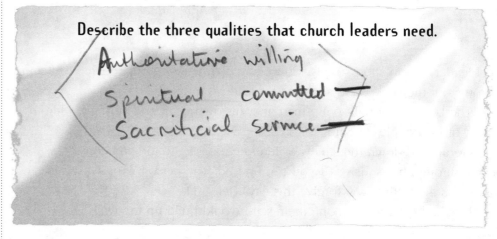

Describe the three qualities that church leaders need.

Authoritative willing
Spiritual   committed
Sacrificial service

Churches grow in every way when they are guided by strong spiritual leaders with the touch of the supernatural radiating in their service. The church sinks into confusion and malaise without such leadership. Today those who preach with majesty and spiritual power are few, and the booming voice of the church has become a pathetic whisper. Leaders today—those who are truly spiritual— must pass on the torch to younger people as a first-line duty.

Many people regard leaders as naturally gifted with intellect, personal forcefulness, and enthusiasm. Such qualities certainly enhance leadership potential, but they do not define the spiritual leader. True leaders must be willing to suffer for the sake of objectives great enough to demand their wholehearted obedience.

Spiritual leaders are not elected, appointed, or created by synods or churchly assemblies. God alone makes them. One does not become a spiritual leader merely by filling an office, taking course work in the subject, or resolving in one's own will to do this task. A person must qualify to be a spiritual leader.

Who calls and makes spiritual leaders?

Often truly authoritative leadership falls on someone who years earlier sought to practice the discipline of seeking first the kingdom of God. Then, as that person matures, God confers a leadership role, and the Spirit of God goes to work through him. When God's searching eye finds a person qualified to lead, God anoints that person with the Holy Spirit and calls him or her to a special ministry (Acts 9:17; 22:21).

Samuel Brengle, a gifted leader who served for many years in the Salvation Army, outlined the road to spiritual authority and leadership:

> It is not won by promotion, but by many prayers and tears. It is attained by confession of sin, and much heartsearching and humbling before God; by self-surrender, a courageous sacrifice of every idol, a bold, uncomplaining embrace of the cross, and by an eternal, unfaltering looking unto Jesus crucified. It is not gained by seeking great things for ourselves, but like Paul, by counting those things that are gain to us as loss for Christ. This is a great price, but it must be paid by the leader who would not be merely a nominal but a real spiritual leader of men, a leader whose power is recognized and felt in heaven, on earth, and in hell.[3]

In the quote from Samuel Brengle, circle the actions he lists as leading to spiritual authority and leadership.

List each of the actions and evaluate these qualities in your own life as a leader.
Use this scale—I do this: Never, Seldom, Regularly, Always

	Never	Seldom	Regularly	Always
1.	___	___	___	___
2.	___	___	___	___
3.	___	___	___	___
4.	___	___	___	___
5.	___	___	___	___
6.	___	___	___	___
7.	___	___	___	___

God wants to show such people how strong He really is (2 Chron. 16:9). But not all who aspire to leadership are willing to pay such a high personal price. Yet there is no compromise here: in the secret reaches of the heart this price is paid, before any public office or honor. Our Lord made clear to James and John that high position in the kingdom of God is reserved for those whose hearts—even the secret places where no one else probes—are qualified. God's sovereign searching of our hearts and then His call to leadership are awesome to behold. And they make a person very humble.

One last thing must be said, a kind of warning. If those who hold influence over others fail to lead toward the spiritual uplands, then surely the path to the lowlands will be well worn. People travel together; no one lives detached and alone.

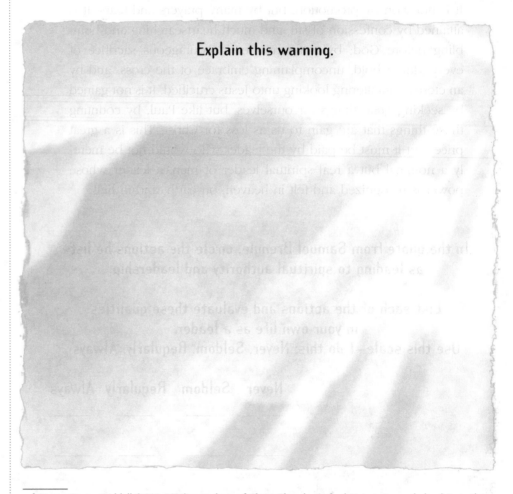

Explain this warning.

---

[1] Henry George Liddell (1811–1898) was dean of Christ Church, Oxford University, and chaplain to the Queen. Lewis Carroll wrote *Alice in Wonderland* for Liddell's daughter Alice.

[2] Quoted in Paul E. Sangster, *Doctor Sangster* (London: Epworth, 1962), 109. William Sangster (1900–1960) was a leader in British Methodism.

[3] Samuel Logan Brengle, *The Soul-Winner's Secret* (London: Salvation Army, 1918), 22.

The Master's Master Principle

Whoever wants to become great among you must be your servant, and whoever wants to be first must be slave of all.

—Mark 10:43-44

Given the importance of competent leaders in the church—and in business and government, too—we might expect that the Bible would use the term more often. In fact, the King James Bible (on which many of my generation have been nurtured) uses the term *leader* only six times. Much more frequently, the role is called *servant*. We do not read about "Moses, my leader," but "Moses, my servant." And this is exactly what Christ taught.[1]

Jesus was a revolutionary, not in the guerrilla warfare sense, but in His teaching on leadership. The term *servant* speaks everywhere of low prestige, low respect, low honor. Most people are not attracted to such a low-value role. When Jesus used the term, however, it was a synonym for greatness. And that was a revolutionary idea.

Christ taught that the kingdom of God is a community where each member serves the others. Paul wrote in the same vein: "Serve one another in love" (Gal. 5:13). Our loving service should spread also to the needy world around us. But in most churches, a few people carry the load.

Jesus knew that the idea of leader as "loving servant of all" would not appeal to most people. Securing our own creature comforts is a much more common mission. But "servant" is His requirement for those who want to lead in His kingdom.

What challenges you the most about being a servant leader?

Overcoming the worldly thoughts of attaining self desires

Time
Selfness
Fear of being rejected

The sharp contrast between our common ideas about leadership and the revolution Jesus announced is nowhere clearer than in Mark 10:42-43: "You know that those who are regarded as rulers of the Gentiles lord it over them, and their high officials exercise authority over them. Not so with you. Instead, whoever wants to become great among you must be your servant, and whoever wants to be first must be slave of all."

This was such a revolutionary idea that even those closest to Jesus, the disciples James and John, used their ambitious mother in a scheme to secure top positions in the coming kingdom before the other ten received their due. These two disciples took seriously Jesus' promise about sitting on glorious thrones and judging the tribes of Israel (Matt. 19:28), but they misunderstood how to get there.

Despite their friendship, Jesus did not give an inch to their campaign for office. "You don't know what you are asking," was His reply (Matt. 20:22). James and John wanted the glory, but not the cup of shame; the crown, but not the cross; the role of master, but not servant. Jesus used this occasion to teach two principles of leadership the church must never forget.

• *The sovereignty of spiritual leadership.* "To sit at my right or left is not for me to grant. These places belong to those for whom they have been prepared" (Mark 10:40).

A more common response might have been: Honor and rank are for those who have prepared themselves for them and worked very hard to get them. But here we see the fundamental difference between Jesus' teaching and our human ideas. God assigns places of spiritual ministry and leadership in His sovereign will. The *Good News Bible* translates verse 40: "It is God who will give these places to those for whom he has prepared them."

Effective spiritual leadership does not come as a result of theological training or seminary degree, as important as education is. Jesus told His disciples, "You did not choose me, but I chose you and appointed you" (John 15:16). The sovereign selection of God gives great confidence to Christian workers. We can truly say, "I am here neither by selection of an individual nor election of a group, but by the almighty appointment of God."

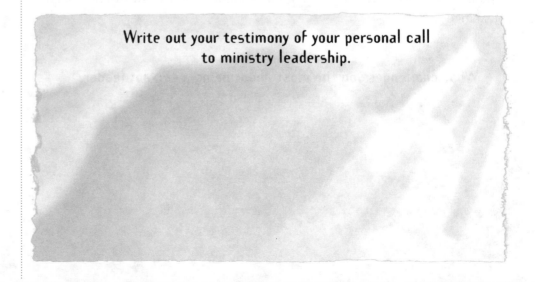

Write out your testimony of your personal call to ministry leadership.

- *The suffering of spiritual leadership.* "Can you drink the cup I drink and be baptized with the baptism I am baptized with?" (Mark 10:38).

No hedging here. No dodging the hard realities. Jesus simply and honestly set forth the cost of serving in His kingdom. The task was magnificent and difficult; men and women leading in that task must have eyes wide open and hearts willing to follow the Master all the way.

To the Lord's probing question, the disciples responded glibly, "We are able." What tragic lack of perspective! But Jesus knew what lay ahead. They would indeed drink the cup and know the baptism. James would be executed, and John would finish His days in isolated confinement.

If the disciples figured to learn about leadership on the fast track and with appropriate perks and bonuses, Jesus soon disillusioned them. What a shock it was to discover that greatness comes through servanthood, and leadership through becoming a slave of all.

Only once in all the recorded words of Jesus did our Lord announce that He would provide an "example" for the disciples, and then He washed their feet (John 13:15). Only once in the rest of the New Testament does a writer offer an "example" (1 Pet. 2:21), and that is an example of suffering. Serving and suffering are paired in the teaching and life of our Lord. One does not come without the other. And what servant is greater than the Lord?

Recap the two principles of leadership
that Jesus taught in Mark 10:40-45:

The __sovereignty__ of spiritual leadership . . .

The __suffering__ of spiritual leadership . . .

The Spirit of Servanthood

Jesus' teaching on servanthood and suffering was not intended merely to inspire good behavior. Jesus wanted to impart the spirit of servanthood, the sense of personal commitment and identity that He expressed when He said, "I am among you as one who serves" (Luke 22:27). Mere acts of service could be performed with motives far from spiritual.

Give an example that illustrates the above statement
regarding acts of service.

In Isaiah 42, we read about the attitudes and inner motives that the coming Messiah would demonstrate as the ideal servant of the Lord. Where Israel failed to live up to this ideal, the Messiah would succeed. And the principles of His life would be a pattern for ours.

Dependence.—"Here is my servant, whom I uphold" (Isa. 42:1). This verse speaks of the coming Messiah. Jesus fulfilled the prophecy by emptying Himself of divine prerogative ("made himself nothing," Phil. 2:7). He surrendered the privileges of His God-nature and became dependent on His heavenly Father. He fully identified Himself with our humanity. What a staggering paradox. As we become "empty" of self and dependent on God, the Holy Spirit will use us.

Approval.—"My chosen one in whom I delight" (Isa. 42:1). God took great delight in His servant Jesus. And that delight was reciprocal. In another Old Testament reference to the coming Messiah, the Son testifies, "I delight to do Thy will, O my God" (Ps. 40:8, KJV).

Modesty.—"He will not shout or cry out, or raise his voice in the streets" (Isa. 42:2). Neither strident nor flamboyant, God's servant conducts a ministry that appears almost self-effacing. What a contrast to the arrogant self-advertising of so many hypesters today, both in and out of the church.

On this very point the devil tempted Jesus, urging Him to attempt a headline-grabbing leap from the rooftop of the temple (Matt. 4:5). But Jesus did not seek headlines and did not fall to the plot.

So quiet and unobtrusive is the great Servant's work that many today doubt His very existence. Jesus exemplifies the description of God found later in Isaiah: "Truly you are a God who hides himself" (Isa. 45:15). This quality seems to be shared among all the host of heaven. Even the picture given to us of the cherubim—God's angel servants—uses four of their six wings to conceal their faces and feet. They, too, are content with hidden service (Isa. 6:2).

Empathy.—"A bruised reed he will not break, and a smoldering wick he will not snuff out" (Isa. 42:3). The Lord's servant is sympathetic with the weak, mercifully understanding toward those who err. How often do people who fail wear the tread marks of fellow pilgrims. But the ideal Servant does not run over the weak and failing. He mends bruises and fans the weak spirit into a flame.

Many of us, even Christian workers, see a person whose life is a wreck and "pass by on the other side." We seek a ministry more rewarding and worthy of our talents than bearing up the frail side of humanity. But from God's point of view, it is noble work to reclaim the world's downtrodden people.

How dimly Peter's own wick burned in the judgment hall, but what a blaze on the day of Pentecost! God's ideal Servant made that miserable man's life a brilliant flame.

Optimism.—"He will not falter or be discouraged till he establishes justice on earth" (Isa. 42:4). Pessimism and leadership are at opposite ends of life's attitudes. Hope and optimism are essential qualities for the servant of God who battles with the powers of darkness over the souls of men and women. God's ideal Servant is optimistic until every part of God's work is done.

Anointing.—"I will put my Spirit on him" (Isa. 42:1). None of these leadership qualities—dependence, approval, modesty, empathy, and optimism—are sufficient for the task. Without the touch of the supernatural, these qualities are dry as dust. And so the Holy Spirit comes to rest upon and dwell in the ideal Servant. "You know. . . how God anointed Jesus of Nazareth with the Holy Spirit and power, and how he went around doing good" (Acts 10:37a, 38). Jesus' ministry began when the Spirit descended at His baptism, and then how the Servant began to shake the world!

Think about your servant leadership attitudes.

Using this scale (1 = very low; 2 = low; 3 = fair; 4 = high; 5 = very high), rank your spiritual leadership attitudes:

* Dependence	1	2	3	4	5
* Approval	1	2	3	4	5
* Modesty	1	2	3	4	5
* Optimism	1	2	3	4	5
* Anointing	1	2	3	4	5

Are we greater than our Lord? Can we do effective ministry without the Spirit of God working through us at every step? God offers us the same anointing. May we follow close to the great Servant and receive the Spirit who shows us more of the Master.

What changes do you see happening in your ministry if you truly seek the Spirit of God in every step you take?

---

[1] Paul S. Rees, "The Community Clue," *Life of Faith*, 26 September 1976, 3.

Natural and Spiritual Leadership

When I came to you. . . my message and my preaching were not with wise and persuasive words, but with a demonstration of the Spirit's power.

—1 Corinthians 2:1*a*, 4

Leadership is influence, the ability of one person to influence others to follow his or her lead. Famous leaders have always known this.

The great military leader Bernard Montgomery spoke of leadership in these terms: "Leadership is the capacity and will to rally men and women to a common purpose, and the character which inspires confidence."[1] An outstanding example of this statement is Sir Winston Churchill, leader of Britain during World War II.

Fleet Admiral Nimitz said: "Leadership may be defined as that quality that inspires sufficient confidence in subordinates as to be willing to accept his views and carry out his commands."

General Charles Gordon once asked Li Hung Chang, a leader in China, two questions: "What is leadership? And how is humanity divided?" Li Hung replied: "There are only three kinds of people—those who are immovable, those who are movable, and those who move them!"

John R. Mott, a world leader in student circles, believed that "a leader is a man who knows the road, who can keep ahead, and who pulls others after him."[2]

P. T. Chandapilla, an Indian student leader, defined Christian leadership as a vocation which blends both human and divine qualities in a harmony of ministry by God and His people for the blessing of others.[3]

Harry S. Truman (U.S. president, 1945–53) said cogently: "A leader is a person who has the ability to get others to do what they don't want to do, and like it."

Spiritual leadership blends natural and spiritual qualities. Yet even the natural qualities are supernatural gifts, since all good things come from God. Take personality, for instance. Montgomery said that "the degree of influence will depend on the personality, the 'incandescence' of which he is capable, the flame which burns within, the magnetism which will draw the hearts of others toward him."[4] Both natural and spiritual qualities reach their greatest effectiveness when employed in the service of God and for His glory.

**What "natural" abilities do you have
which help you as a church leader?**

*Make decisions
Take Consequences good or bad
Love for people
Love to see them grow*

With what spiritual gifts have you been blessed?

*prophecy
teaching*

Yet spiritual leadership transcends the power of personality and all other natural gifts. The personality of the spiritual leader influences others because it is irradiated, penetrated, and empowered by the Holy Spirit. As the leader gives control of his life to the Spirit, the Spirit's power flows through him to others.

Spiritual leadership requires superior spiritual power, which can never be generated by the self. There is no such thing as a self-made spiritual leader. A true leader influences others spiritually only because the Spirit works in and through him to a greater degree than in those he leads.

**Taking into consideration both your natural and spiritual gifts,
what is the key ingredient to spiritual leadership?**

_____

We can lead others only as far along the road as we ourselves have traveled. Merely pointing the way is not enough. If we are not walking, then no one can be following, and we are not leading anyone.

**Rewrite and personalize the above thought
in regard to your own ministry.**

We have to live it before we can lead it. Our walk is the key element in our leading.

At a large meeting of mission leaders in China, the discussion turned to leadership and its qualifications. The debate was vigorous. But through it all, one person sat quietly listening. Then the chair asked if D. E. Hoste, general director of China Inland Mission, had an opinion. The auditorium became still.

With a twinkle in his eye, Hoste said in his high-pitched voice: "It occurs to me that perhaps the best test of whether one is qualified to lead, is to find out whether anyone is following."[5]

Born or Made?

Are leaders born or made? Surely, both. On the one hand, leadership is an "elusive and electric quality" that comes directly from God. On the other, leadership skills are distributed widely among every community and should be cultivated and developed. Often our skills lie dormant until a crisis arises.

Some people become leaders by luck and timing. A crisis comes, no one better qualified steps forward, and a leader is born. Yet closer investigation usually reveals that the selection was not accidental but was more the result of hidden training that made the person fit for leadership. Joseph is a perfect example. He became prime minister of Egypt through circumstances that most people would call "lucky stars." In fact his promotion was the outcome of 13 years of rigorous, hidden training under the hand of God.

When we contrast natural and spiritual leadership, we see just how different they are.

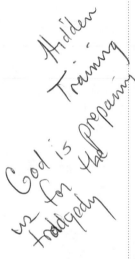

Natural	Spiritual
Self-confident	Confident in God
Knows men	Also knows God
Makes own decisions	Seeks God's will
Ambitious	Humble
Creates methods	Follows God's example
Enjoys command	Delights in obedience to God
Seeks personal reward	Loves God and others
Independent	Depends on God

People without natural leadership skills do not become great leaders at the moment of conversion. Yet a review of the history of the church reveals that the Holy Spirit sometimes releases gifts and qualities that were dormant beforehand. When that happens, a leader is born.

A. W. Tozer wrote:

> A true and safe leader is likely to be one who has no desire to lead, but is forced into a position by the inward pressure of the Holy Spirit and the press of [circumstances]. . . . There was hardly a great leader from Paul to the present day but was drafted by the Holy Spirit for the task, and commissioned by the Lord to fill a position he had little heart for. . . . The man who is ambitious to lead is disqualified as a leader. The true leader will have no desire to lord it over God's heritage, but will be humble, gentle, self-sacrificing and altogether ready to follow when the Spirit chooses another to lead.[6]

Sangster's biography includes a private manuscript written when the English preacher and scholar felt a growing conviction to take more of a leadership role in the Methodist church.

This is the will of God for me. I did not choose it. I sought to escape it. But it has come.

Something else has come, too. A sense of certainty that God does not want me only for a preacher. He wants me also for a leader—a leader in Methodism.

I feel a commissioning to work under God for the revival of this branch of His Church [Methodist]—careless of my own reputation; indifferent to the comments of older and jealous men.

I am thirty-six. If I am to serve God is this way, I must no longer shrink from the task—but *do* it.

I have examined my heart for ambition. I am certain it is not there. I hate the criticism I shall evoke and the painful chatter of people. Obscurity, quiet browsing among books, and the service of simple people is my taste—but by the will of God, this is my task, God help me.

Bewildered and unbelieving, I hear the voice of God say to me: "I want to sound the note through you." O God, did ever an apostle shrink from his task more? I dare not say "no" but, like Jonah, I would fain run away.[7]

Once Saint Francis of Assisi was confronted by a brother who asked him repeatedly, "Why you? Why you?"

Francis responded, in today's terms, "Why me *what?*"

"Why does everyone want to see you? hear you? obey you? You are not all so handsome, nor learned, nor from a noble family. Yet the world seems to want to follow you," the brother said.

Then Francis raised his eyes to heaven, knelt in praise to God, and turned to his interrogator:

You want to know? It is because the eyes of the Most High have willed it so. He continually watches the good and the wicked, and as His most holy eyes have not found among sinners any smaller man, nor any more insufficient and sinful, therefore He has chosen me to accomplish the marvelous work which God hath undertaken; He chose me because He could find none more worthless, and He wished to confound the nobility and grandeur, the strength, the beauty and the learning of this world.[8]

Bernard Montgomery outlined seven qualities necessary for a military leader, each appropriate to spiritual warfare: The leader must (1) avoid getting swamped in detail; (2) not be petty; (3) not be pompous; (4) know how to select people to fit the task; (5) trust others to do a job without the leader's meddling; (6) be capable of clear decisions; (7) inspire confidence.[9]

Circle any qualities in Montgomery's list which are weak areas in your leadership skills.

John Mott moved in student circles, and his tests covered different territory. One should inquire of a leader whether he or she (1) does little things well; (2) has learned to focus on priorities; (3) uses leisure well; (4) has intensity; (5) knows how to exploit momentum; (6) is growing; (7) overcomes discouragement and "impossible" situations; and (8) understands his or her weaknesses.[10]

Choose one area from Mott's list that you need to develop.

_____

A single life has immense possibilities for good or ill. We leave an indelible influence on people who come within our influence, even when we are not aware of it. Dr. John Geddie went to Aneityum in 1848 and worked there for 24 years. Written in his memory are these words:

When he landed, in 1848, there were no Christians.

When he left, in 1872, there were no heathen.[11]

When the burning zeal of the early church began to draw converts at an extraordinary rate, the Holy Spirit taught a wonderful lesson on leadership. The church had too few leaders to care for all the needs, especially among the poor and the widows. Another echelon of leaders was needed. "Brothers, choose seven men from among you who are known to be full of the Spirit and wisdom. We will turn this responsibility over to them" (Acts 6:3).

These new leaders were first and foremost to be full of the Spirit. Spirituality is not easy to define, but you can tell when it is present. It is the fragrance of the garden of the Lord, the power to change the atmosphere around you, the influence that makes Christ real to others.

If deacons are required to be full of the Spirit, should those who preach and teach the Word of God be any less? Spiritual goals can be achieved only by spiritual people who use spiritual methods. How our churches and mission agencies would change if leaders were Spirit-filled! The secular mind and heart, however gifted and personally charming, has no place in the leadership of the church.

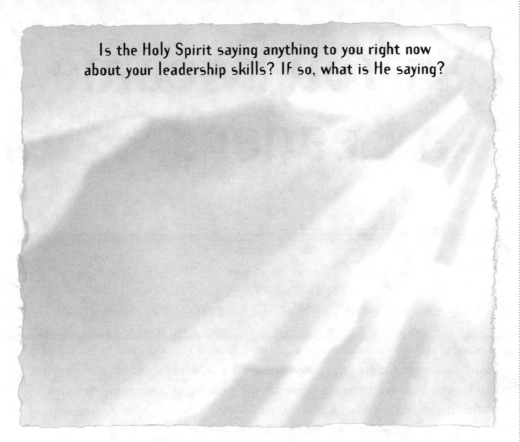

Is the Holy Spirit saying anything to you right now about your leadership skills? If so, what is He saying?

John Mott captured well the heart of spiritual leadership:

> Leadership in the sense of rendering maximum service; leadership in the sense of the largest unselfishness; in the sense of full-hearted absorption in the greatest work of the world: building up the kingdom of our Lord Jesus Christ.[12]

[1] Bernard L. Montgomery, *Memoirs of Field-Marshal Montgomery* (Cleveland: World, 1958), 70. Bernard Law Montgomery (1887–1976) made his mark in World War II as the first allied general to inflict a decisive defeat on the Axis, at El Alamein in Northern Africa, in October 1942. He was knighted that November.

Chester Nimitz (1885–1966), quoted in Sanders's text without a citation, was commander of the Pacific Fleet and Pacific Ocean Areas during World War II.

Charles George Gordon (1833–85), also quoted without citation, was an eccentric but effective British military commander in China during the 1860s (for which he was tagged "Chinese Gordon") and in Africa, where he died at Khartoum trying to withstand an overwhelming army led by the Mahdi, a mystic leader in the Sudan

[2] Lettie B. Cowman, *Charles E. Cowman* (Los Angeles: Oriental Missionary Society, 1928), 251. John R. Mott (1865–1955) was a Methodist evangelist who served in the Student Volunteer Movement and the YMCA. His best-known book is *Evangelizing the World in Our Generation* (1900), which was also the motto he was widely known for. He was a founder of the World Council of Churches.

[3] P. T. Chandapilla was general secretary for the Union of Evangelical Students of India (1956–71.) His goal was to reach India's intellectuals with the gospel. Following Hudson Taylor, Chandapilla never asked for financial help. He worked closely with InterVarsity Fellowship and the International Fellowship of Evangelical Students.

[4] Montgomery, 70.

[5] Phyllis Thompson, *D. E. Hoste* (London: China Inland Mission, n.d.), 122.

[6] A. W. Tozer, in *The Reaper,* February 1962, 459. Aiden Wilson Tozer (1897-1963) was a minister in the Christian and Missionary Alliance. Among his 30 books, the best known is *The Pursuit of God* (1948).

[7] Paul E. Sangster, *Doctor Sangster* (London: Epworth, 1962), 109.

[8] James Burns, *Revivals, Their Laws and Leaders* (London: Hodder & Stoughton, 1909), 95. The text in this quotation has been modernized.

[9] Montgomery, 70.

[10] B. Matthews, *John R. Mott* (London: S.C.M. Press, 1934), 346.

[11] John Geddie (1815–72), born in Scotland, was called the father of foreign missions in the Presbyterian church in Canada. He went as a missionary to the New Hebrides (formerly called Aneityum) in 1848.

[12] Matthews, 353.

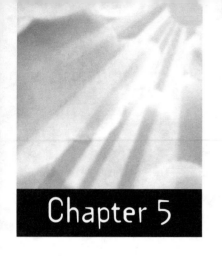

Can You Become a Leader?

Chapter 5

Send some men to explore the land of Canaan. . . .
From each ancestral tribe send one of its leaders.

—Numbers 13:2

When Jesus selected leaders, He ignored every popular idea of His day (and ours) about what kind of person could fit the role. Jesus' band of disciples was untrained and without influence—a motley group for world change.

Any campaign for change today would have a star-studded cast of directors and advisers. In Jesus' group, where was the prominent statesman, the financier, the athlete, the professor, or the acclaimed clergy? Instead, Jesus looked for a humbler sort of person, unspoiled by the sophistication of His day.

Jesus chose from the ranks of workers, not professional clergy. When Hudson Taylor did the same thing, selecting mostly lay men and women for his missionary team to China, the religious world was shocked. Today that is a widely recognized, though not always approved, procedure.

Jesus chose people with little education, but they soon displayed remarkable flair. He saw in them something no one else did, and under His skillful hand they emerged as leaders who would shock the world. To their latent talents were added fervent devotion and fierce loyalty, honed in the school of failure and fatigue.

Natural leadership qualities are important. Too often these skills lie dormant and undiscovered. If we look carefully, we should be able to detect leadership potential. And if we have it, we should train it and use it for Christ's work. Here are some ways to investigate your potential:

- Have you ever broken a bad habit? To lead others, you must master your appetites.
- Do you keep self-control when things go wrong? The leader who loses control under adversity forfeits respect and influence. A leader must be calm in crisis and resilient in disappointment.
- Do you think independently? A leader must use the best ideas of others to make decisions. A leader cannot wait for others to make up his or her mind.
- Can you handle criticism? Can you profit from it? The humble person can learn from petty criticism, even malicious criticism.
- Can you turn disappointment into creative new opportunity?
- Do you readily gain the cooperation of others and win their respect and confidence?

※ • Can you exert discipline without making a power play? True leadership is an internal quality of the spirit and needs no show of external force.

※ • Are you a peacemaker? A leader must be able to reconcile with opponents and make peace where arguments have created hostility.

※ • Do people trust you with difficult and delicate situations?

※ • Can you induce people to do happily some legitimate thing that they would not normally wish to do?

+ • Can you accept opposition to your viewpoint or decision without taking offense? Leaders always face opposition.

※ • Can you make and keep friends? Your circle of loyal friends is an index of your leadership potential.

※ • Do you depend on the praise of others to keep you going? Can you hold steady in the face of disapproval and even temporary loss of confidence?

※ • Are you at ease in the presence of strangers? Do you get nervous in the presence of your superior?

※ • Are the people who report to you generally at ease? A leader should be sympathetic and friendly.

※ • Are you interested in people? All types? All races? No prejudice?

※ • Are you tactful? Can you anticipate how your words will affect a person?

※ • Is your will strong and steady? Leaders cannot vacillate or cannot drift with the wind.

+ • Can you forgive? Or do you nurse resentments and harbor ill-feelings toward those who have injured you?

※ • Are you reasonably optimistic? Pessimism and leadership do not mix.

※ • Do you feel a master passion such as that of Paul, who said, "This one thing I do!" Such a singleness of motive will focus your energies and powers on the desired objective. Leaders need a strong focus.

※ • Do you welcome responsibility?

Mark the above leadership traits as follows:
+ A trait I have but have not developed
* A well-developed trait I have
– A trait I do not have

How we handle relationships tells a lot about our potential for leadership. R. E. Thompson suggests these tests:

- Do other people's failures annoy or challenge you?
- Do you "use" people, or cultivate people?
- Do you direct people, or develop people?
- Do you criticize, or encourage?
- Do you shun or seek out the person with a special need or problem?[1]

Circle any of the relationship qualities which you need to strengthen.

These tests mean little unless we act to correct our deficits and fill in the gaps of our training. Perhaps the final test of leadership potential is whether you "sit" on the results of such an analysis or do something about them. Why not take some of the points of weakness and failure you are aware of and in cooperation with the Holy Spirit, who is the Spirit of discipline, concentrate on strengthening those areas of weakness and correcting faults?

Desirable qualities were present in all their fullness in the character of our Lord. Each Christian should make it his constant prayer that they might more rapidly be incorporated into his own personality.

Under the guidance of the Holy Spirit, prepare a list of ways to strengthen your weak leadership traits.

What does God want you to do in response to this material?

Adding leadership potential to our lives usually requires that we shake off negative elements that hold us back. If we are overly sensitive when criticized and rush to defend ourselves, that must go. If we make excuses for failure and try to blame others or circumstances, that must go. If we are intolerant or inflexible so that creative people around us feel hemmed in, that must go.

If we are disturbed by anything short of perfection in ourselves and others, that must go. The perfectionist sets goals beyond his reach, then sinks into false guilt when he falls short. Our world is imperfect, and we cannot expect the impossible. Setting modest, realistic goals will help a perfectionist move through a problem without discouragement.

If you cannot keep a secret, do not try to lead. If you cannot yield a point when someone else's ideas are better, save yourself the frustration of failed leadership. If you want to maintain an image of infallibility, find something else to do besides leading people.

---

[1] R. E. Thompson, in *World Vision,* December 1966, 4.

Insights on Leadership from Paul

Now the overseer must be above reproach, the husband of but one wife, temperate, self-controlled, respectable, hospitable, able to teach, not given to drunkenness, not violent but gentle, not quarrelsome, not a lover of money. He must manage his own family well and see that his children obey him with proper respect. . . . He must not be a recent convert, or he may become conceited. . . . He must also have a good reputation with outsiders.

—1 Timothy 3:2-4, 6-7

Underline each quality Paul lists as a requirement for church leadership.

A friend once said to me, "Isn't it humbling to see your own faults running around on two little legs!" The comment reminded me of how much clearer are spiritual principles when we see them "running around," instead of merely stating them in the abstract. The apostle Paul embodied principles of leadership that he also described in his letters. Looking at his life, we can see leadership all the more clearly.

The reputation of a great leader grows with the years. Surely Paul's moral and spiritual greatness is all the more evident the more he is studied and analyzed. A. W. Tozer called him the world's most successful Christian. It is sheer irony and miracle that God would select one of the most aggressive opponents of the early Christian movement and make him into its most outstanding leader.

Paul was uniquely equipped for the major role to which God called him. A present-day parallel to this amazing man would be someone who could speak in Chinese in Beijing, quoting Confucius and Mencius; write cogent theology, and teach it at Oxford; and defend his cause using flawless Russian before the Soviet Academy of Sciences. By whatever comparison, Paul was certainly one of the most versatile leaders the church has known.

His versatility is apparent in the ease with which he adapted to various audiences. Paul could address statesmen and soldiers, adults and children, kings and royal officials. He was at ease in debate with philosophers, theologians, and pagan idol worshipers.

Paul had a brilliant grasp of the Old Testament. He studied under the influential rabbi Gamaliel, and as a student Paul was second to none. His own testimony records: "I was advancing in Judaism beyond many Jews of my own age and was extremely zealous for the traditions of my fathers" (Gal. 1:14).

A natural leader by any measure, Paul became a great spiritual leader when his heart and mind were captured by Jesus Christ.

Paul had boundless, Christ-centered ambition. His supreme love for Christ coupled with the obligation to share Christ's message were his powerful lifetime motives (Rom. 1:14; 2 Cor. 5:14). His authentic missionary passion helped him leap over all cultural and racial barriers. All people were his concern. A person's wealth or poverty, social status or intellect had no bearing on Paul's concern for him.

In addition to his own schooling and experiences, Paul enjoyed the illumination and inspiration of the Holy Spirit. The qualities of leadership Paul taught are as relevant now as during the first century A.D. We dare not toss them off as antiquated or carelessly regard them as mere options.

List the qualifications you had to meet for your present position.

Circle any of the above qualifications that are also found in Paul's list of church leader qualifications.

In your opinion, is Paul's list of qualifications for church leaders relevant for today's church leaders? Why or why not?

The selection from 1 Timothy quoted at the head of this chapter spells out qualifications for spiritual leadership. Let us look at it again, and consider its parts.

Social Qualifications

With respect to relationships within the church, the leader is to be above reproach. Detractors should not have a rung to stand on. If a charge is preferred against the leader, it would fail because his life would afford no grounds for reproach or indictment of wrongdoing. His adversary finds no opening for a smear campaign, rumor mongering, or gossip.

> **Analyze your relationship within the church.**
> **Are there persons with whom you have problems? Identify persons and the steps you will take to improve these relationships.**

With respect to relationships outside the church, the spiritual leader is to enjoy a good reputation. An elder known to the author was a businessman who often took preaching appointments on the Lord's Day. His employees used to say that they could tell when he had been preaching on Sunday because of his ill-temper on Monday. Those outside the church can see plainly when our lives fall short of our testimony. We cannot hope to lead people to Christ by living an example of such contradiction.

Outsiders will criticize; nonetheless, they respect the high ideals of Christian character. When a Christian leader full of high ideals lives a holy and joyful life in front of unbelievers, they will want to cultivate a similar experience. The character of the elder should command the respect of the unbeliever, inspire his confidence, and arouse his aspiration. Example is much more potent than precept.

> **Complete this sentence:**
> **In my community I have the reputation for being . . .**

Moral Qualifications

Moral principles common to the Christian life are under constant, subtle attack, and none more so than sexual faithfulness. The Christian leader must be blameless on this vital and often unpopular point. Faithfulness to one marriage partner is the biblical norm. The spiritual leader should be a man of unchallengeable morality.

The spiritual leader must be temperate, not addicted to alcohol. To be drunk is to show a disorderly personal life. Drink is a disgrace anywhere, and much more so when it captures a Christian. A leader cannot allow a secret indulgence that would undermine public witness.

What steps do you recommend church leaders take to avoid putting themselves into compromising situations?

Mental Qualifications

A leader must be prudent, a person with sound judgment. This principle describes "the well-balanced state of mind resulting from habitual self-restraint"—the inner character that comes from daily self-discipline. Jeremy Taylor called this quality "reason's girdle and passion's bridle."[1] The ancient Greeks, who valued this quality, described it as a disciplined mind not swayed by sudden impulse or flying to extremes. For example, courage to the Greeks was the "golden mean" between rashness and timidity; purity was the mean between prudery and immorality. In a similar way, the Christian leader who possesses a sound mind has control of every part of his or her personality, habits, and passions.

If you took this statement ("The Christian leader who possesses a sound mind has control of every part of his or her personality, habits, and passions") seriously, what changes would you need to make in your life?

As to behavior, the leader must be respectable. A well-ordered life is the fruit of a well-ordered mind. The life of the leader should reflect the beauty and orderliness of God.

Then the leader must be ready and able to teach. In a leader, watch for this desire, this spark. It creates opportunities to help others understand the meaning of spiritual life. The leader feels the joy of the Spirit and wants others to know God as well. Moreover, the leader's responsibility for teaching those under him should be supported by a blameless life.

Teaching is hard work; and doing it well takes time, preparation, study, and prayer.

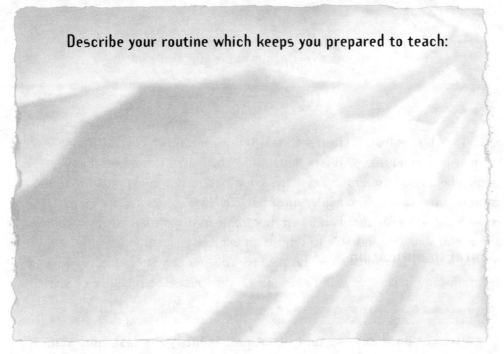

Describe your routine which keeps you prepared to teach:

Samuel Brengle lamented:

> Oh, for teachers among us; leaders who know how to read hearts and apply truth to the needs of the people, as a good physician reads patients and applies remedies to their ills. There are soul-sicknesses open and obscure, acute and chronic, superficial and deep-seated which the truth in Jesus will heal. But it is not the same truth for each need, any more than the same medicine for every disease. That is why we should most diligently study the Bible and pray for the constant and powerful illumination of the Spirit.[2]

John Wesley had these gifts. He never indulged in a cheap disparagement of the intellect and was always trying to promote knowledge of the Scriptures and spiritual renewal among the people. He was intellectually gifted and possessed an impressive command of English literature. An eminent preacher declared that he knew of no sermons that gave greater evidence of an intimate knowledge of classical and general literature than those of Wesley. Yet he was widely known as a person "of one Book." That kind of breadth, focused on the Scriptures, is a high example of the consecrated intellect of the spiritual leader.

Personality Qualifications

If you would rather pick a fight than solve a problem, do not consider leading the church. The Christian leader must be genial and gentle, not a lover of controversy.

What areas seem to put you into "controversy"?

R. C. Trench says that the leader should be one who corrects and "redresses the injustices of justice." Aristotle taught that the leader should be one who "remembers good rather than evil, the good one has received rather than the good one has done." The leader must be actively considerate, not merely passive and certainly not withdrawn, but irenic in disposition, always seeking a peaceful solution, and able to diffuse an explosive situation.

Then the leader must show hospitality. This ministry should never be seen as an irksome imposition, but rather as one that offers the privilege of service.

Reflect on your hospitality quotient. Identify the last time you:

A. Invited some church members for dinner in your home.

B. Thanked God for the privilege of ministering to others.

C. Served the needy in your community.

D. Entertained fellow ministers in your home.

E. Gave your personal time to a disadvantaged church member.

The Shepherd of Hermas, a widely used book written in the second century A.D., mentions that a bishop "must be hospitable, a man who gladly and at all times welcomes into his house the servants of God."

When Paul wrote his letter to Timothy, inns were few, dirty, and known for their immoral atmosphere. Visiting Christians depended on open doors of hospitality. A friend of the author, a person with a rather large portfolio of business and church responsibilities, kept an "open home" policy for visitors and the underprivileged on each Lord's Day. It was a practice that enriched his life and blessed others, and demonstrated this important quality of spiritual leadership.

Covetousness and its twin, the love of money, disqualify a person for leadership. Financial reward cannot enter a leader's mind in the exercise of ministry. The leader must be as willing to accept an appointment with a lower remuneration as one with a higher.

Before going to Madeley, John Fletcher was told by his benefactor, Mr. Hill, that he could have a position in Dunham in Cheshire, where "the parish is small, the duty light, and the income good." Moreover, it was "in fine sporting country."

"Alas, sir," replied Fletcher, "Dunham will not suit me. There is too much money and too little labor."

"It is a pity to decline such a living," said Hill. "Would you like Madeley?"

"That, sir, would be the very place for me." And in that church the man who cared nothing for money had a remarkable ministry, still being felt in this generation.[3]

Domestic Qualifications

The Christian leader who is married must demonstrate the ability to "manage his own family well and see that his children obey him with proper respect" (1 Tim. 3:4). We cannot accept the picture of a stern, unsmiling patriarch, immune to laughter and impervious to emotion. But Paul urges a well-ordered home where mutual respect and supportive harmony are the keynotes. Failure to keep home in order has kept many ministers and missionaries from their fullest potential.

List the ways you regularly practice to support and undergird your family relationships.

To reach this goal, a spouse must fully share the leader's spiritual aspirations and be willing to join in the necessary sacrifices. Many a gifted leader has been lost to high office and spiritual effectiveness because of an uncooperative spouse. Without a benevolent and happy discipline in one's home, can a Christian worker be expected to manage a ministry? Can hospitality be offered if children carry on without restraint? Can a ministry to other families be effective if one's own family is in disarray?

While a leader is caring for church and mission, he must not neglect the family, which is his primary and personal responsibility. The discharge of one duty in God's kingdom does not excuse us from another. There is time for every legitimate duty. Paul implies that a person's ability to lead at home is a strong indicator of his readiness to lead in ministry.

Maturity

Spiritual maturity is indispensable to good leadership. A novice or new convert should not be pushed into leadership. A plant needs time to take root and come to maturity, and the process cannot be hurried. The seed must take root downward before it can bear fruit upward. J. A. Bengel says that novices usually have "an abundance of [vegetation]" and are "not yet pruned by the cross." In 1 Timothy 3:10, referring to qualifications for deacon, Paul urges, "They must first be tested."

The church in Ephesus was a decade old when Timothy became its pastor. This church had in it a galaxy of gifted teachers, so there were many men of mature experience in it; hence Paul's insistence that the new minister be mature—not as old as the others, but as spiritually rooted and fruitful. Paul did not insist on maturity as a qualification to lead the newly established church at Crete (Titus 1:5-9), where mature members were not yet present. In the early stages of building a church, we cannot insist on maturity, but every care must be taken that those developing the work be stable in character, spiritual in outlook, and not ambitious for position.

Paul warns that a person not ready for leadership, and thrust into the role, "may become conceited and fall under the same judgment as the devil" (1 Tim. 3:6). A new convert does not yet possess the spiritual stability essential to leading people wisely. It is unwise to give key positions too early even to those who manifest promising talent, lest it spoil them.

What warning did Paul give concerning putting immature Christians into leadership positions?

The story of the church and its mission is filled with examples of failed leaders who were appointed too soon. A novice suddenly placed in authority over others faces the danger of inflated ego. Instead, the promising convert should be given a widening opportunity to serve at humbler and less prominent tasks that will develop both natural and spiritual gifts. He should not be advanced too fast, lest he become puffed up. Neither should he be repressed, lest he be discouraged.

Paul did not appoint elders in every place on his first missionary journey. He sometimes waited until a later visit when questions about spiritual development were satisfied (Acts 14:23). Timothy was converted during Paul's first journey, but not ordained until the second journey.[4]

"It is the mark of a grown-up man, as compared with a callow youth, that he finds his center of gravity wherever he happens to be at the moment, and however much he longs for the object of his desire, it cannot prevent him from staying at his post and doing his duty," wrote Dietrich Bonhoeffer.[5] That is just what a new convert finds difficult to do. It is a characteristic that accompanies a growing maturity and stability.

Maturity is shown in a magnanimous spirit and broad vision. Paul's encounter with Christ transformed him from a narrow-minded bigot into a full-hearted leader. The indwelling Christ enlarged his passion for others, broadened his view of the world, and deepened his convictions.

The importance of the above requirements for leadership in the Christian church is recognized even in secular circles. Secular circles recognize the importance of these qualities as much as do churches and missions. The pagan Onosander described the ideal field commander: "He must be prudently self-controlled, sober, frugal, enduring in toil, intelligent, without love of money, neither young nor old, if possible the father of a family, able to speak competently, and of good reputation."[6]

If the world demands such standards of its leaders, the church of the living God should select its leaders with even greater care.

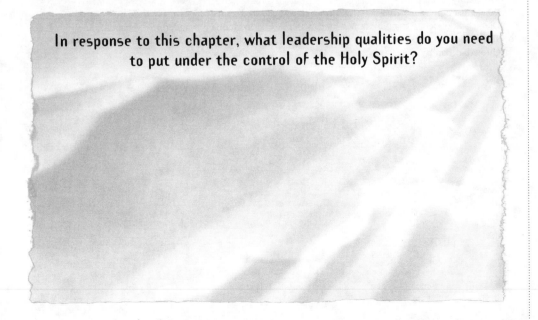

In response to this chapter, what leadership qualities do you need to put under the control of the Holy Spirit?

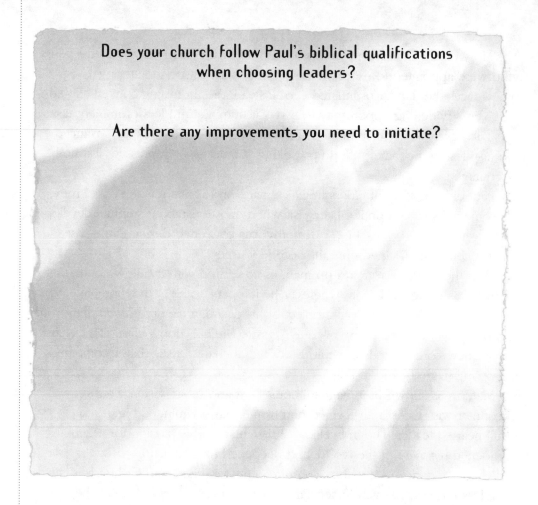

Does your church follow Paul's biblical qualifications
when choosing leaders?

Are there any improvements you need to initiate?

[1] William Barclay, *Letters to Timothy and Titus* (Edinburgh: St. Andrews, 1960), 92. Jeremy Taylor (1613-67) was an Anglican bishop and chaplain to Charles I. He is known today for his devotional writings, especially *Holy Living* (1650) and *Holy Dying* (1651), written after Charles was beheaded and the victorious Oliver Cromwell was at his peak. Taylor was one of the most popular preachers of his day.
Mencius (c. 372–c. 289 B.C.), the Chinese philosopher mentioned without citation in the third paragraph, was Confucius' greatest disciple. He promoted the cardinal virtues of love, righteousness, decorum, and wisdom. His Latinized name comes from Meng-Tzu, meaning Master Meng. He was known as the Second Sage.
[2] C. W. Hall, *Samuel Logan Brengle* (New York: Salvation Army, 1933), 112.
[3] John William Fletcher (1729-85) was vicar of Madeley in Shropshire. Swiss by birth, he joined the Methodist movement within the Church of England. He is remembered for his sanctity and his devotion to work among coal miners.
[4] William Hendriksen, *1 and 2 Timothy and Titus* (London: Banner of Truth, 1959), 36.
[5] Dietrich Bonhoeffer, quoted but not cited, was a leader in Germany's underground church during the Third Reich. He was executed by the Nazis in 1945 just before Allied troops reached his prison camp.
[6] Quoted in Barclay, 86.

Insights on Leadership from Peter

To the elders among you, I appeal as a fellow elder, a witness of Christ's suffering and one who will also share in the glory to be revealed: Be shepherd's of God's flock that is under your care, serving as overseers—not because you must, but because you are willing, as God wants you to be; not greedy for money, but eager to serve; not lording it over those entrusted to you, but being examples to the flock. And when the Chief Shepherd appears, you will receive the crown of glory that will never fade away.

Young men, in the same way be submissive to those who are older. All of you, clothe yourselves with humility toward one another, because, "God opposes the proud, but gives grace to the humble."

Humble yourselves, therefore, under God's mighty hand, that he may lift you up in due time. Cast all your anxiety on him because he cares for you.

—1 Peter 5:1-7

Peter was the natural leader of the apostolic band. What Peter did, the others did; where he went, the others went. His mistakes, which sprang from his impetuous personality, were many; but his influence and leadership were without equal. We do well to ponder the advice of Peter's mature years to spiritual leaders of every generation.

See that your "flock of God" is properly fed and cared for, Peter urges (1 Pet. 5:2). Such is a shepherd's primary responsibility. In these words we can hear the resonance of Peter's never-to-be-forgotten interview with Jesus after his failure, the interview that restored him and assured him of Jesus' continuing love and care (John 21:15-22). Likewise, these "strangers in the world" (1 Pet. 1:1) about whom Peter was writing were themselves passing through deep trials. Peter could feel for them and with them, and he wrote his letter to elders with that in mind.

Peter does not approach his readers from on high, as a virtuoso apostle. Rather, he takes the position of fellow elder, coming alongside the others and bearing similar burdens. He also writes as a witness to the sufferings of Christ, one whose heart has been humbled by failure, broken and conquered by Calvary's love. He is a leader who looks across at others but not down. A shepherd's work requires a shepherd's heart.

First, Peter deals with a leader's motivation. The spiritual leader is to approach the work willingly, not by coercion. Leaders of the church in Peter's day faced challenges that would daunt the stoutest heart, yet Peter urges that they not faint or retreat from them. Nor should leaders serve from a sense of mere duty, but because of love. The work of pastoring and helping new believers to grow is to be done "as God wants," not directed by personal preferences or desires. William Barclay captures the spirit of it:

> Peter says to the leaders, "Shepherd your people *like* God." Just as Israel is God's special allotment, the people we have to serve in the church or anywhere else are our special allotment; and our whole attitude to them must be the attitude of God; we must shepherd them like God. What a vision opens out! What an ideal! And what a condemnation! It is our task to show people the forbearance of God, the forgiveness of God, the seeking love of God, the limitless service of God.[1]

When God calls us, we cannot refuse from a sense of inadequacy. Nobody is worthy of such trust. When Moses tried that excuse, God became angry (Ex. 4:14). Let us not pass the buck of leadership because we think ourselves incapable.

The spiritual leader cannot have money in his eyes when service beckons.—Do not work as one "greedy for money," Peter warns (1 Pet. 5:2). Perhaps Peter had in mind Judas, whose passion for money led to his fall. Leaders will be called upon to formulate policy, to set budgets and decide priorities, to deal with property. None of that can be done well if personal gain looms as a background motive.

Paul Rees suggests that the greed Peter warns against extends beyond money to fame and prestige, which are sometimes a more insidious temptation. Whether for fame or fortune, avarice cannot coexist with leadership in the church.[2]

"I am not sure which of the two occupies the lower sphere, he who hungers for money or he who thirsts for applause," wrote J. H. Jowett. "A preacher may dress and smooth his message to court the public cheers, and labourers in other spheres may bid for prominence, for imposing print, for grateful recognition. All this unfits us for our task. It destroys perception of the needs and perils of the sheep."[3]

The Christian leader must not be dictatorial.—"Not lording it over those entrusted to you" (1 Pet. 5:3). A domineering manner, an unbridled ambition, an offensive strut, a tyrant's talk—no attitude could be less fit for one who claims to be a servant of the Son of God.

A leader must be a worthy example for the people.—"But being examples to the flock" (1 Pet. 5:3). These words remind us of Paul's advice to Timothy: "But set an example for the believers in speech, in life, in love, in faith and in purity" (1 Tim. 4:12). Peter teaches that elders need the shepherd spirit. Should elders ever forget whose flock they lead, Peter reminds them that it is God's. Jesus is the Chief Shepherd; we are assistants and associates working under His authority.

If done "as God wants," then leadership will surely include intercessory prayer. The saintly Bishop Azariah of India once remarked to Bishop Stephen Neill that he found time to pray daily, by name, for every leader in his extensive diocese. Little wonder that during his 30 years of eldering there, the diocese tripled its membership and greatly increased in spiritual effectiveness.[4]

The leader must be clothed "with humility" (1 Pet. 5:5).—The verb refers to a slave's tying on a white apron, which gives this verse an added note of meaning. Was Peter recalling the sad night when he refused to take the towel and wash his master's feet? Would pride keep other leaders from joyful service? Pride ever lurks at the heels of power, but God will not encourage proud men in His service. Rather, He will oppose and obstruct them.

But to the undershepherd who is humble and lowly in heart, God will add power and grace to the work of humble men and women. In verse 5, Peter urged leaders to act humbly in relating to others. But in verse 6 he challenges leaders to react humbly to the discipline of God. Always in the mind of the leader is the merciful and glorious God who extends to us the privilege of serving in His mission field.

Peter concludes this section of teaching with a mention of heavenly reward: "When the Chief Shepherd appears, you will receive the crown of glory that will never fade away" (1 Pet. 5:4). An athlete's crown would wither; even a king's crown would rust. But no such loss comes to the Christian servant who has chosen treasures in heaven over comforts on earth.

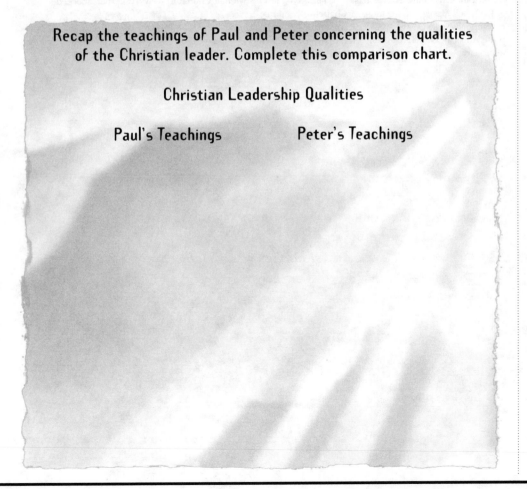

Recap the teachings of Paul and Peter concerning the qualities of the Christian leader. Complete this comparison chart.

Christian Leadership Qualities

Paul's Teachings   Peter's Teachings

Are we alone in the leader's role? Do we work in solitude? Not at all, Peter announces. Rather, our frustrations and worries are shared with God, who offers relief and reprieve. "Cast all your anxiety on him because he cares for you" (1 Pet 5:7). The Christian leader need not fear that care of the flock of God will be too heavy a burden. By God's invitation, the leader can transfer the weight of spiritual burdens onto shoulders bigger, stronger, broader, and more durable. God cares for you. Let worries go!

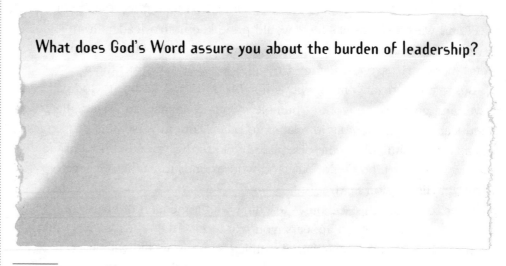

What does God's Word assure you about the burden of leadership?

---

[1] William Barclay, *The Letters of Peter and Jude* (Edinburgh: St. Andrews, 1958), 156.

[2] Paul S. Rees, *Triumphant in Trouble* (London: Marshall, Morgan & Scott, n.d.), 126.

[3] J. H. Jowett, *The Epistles of Peter* (London: Hodder & Stoughton, n.d.), 188. Jowett (1863–1923), an English Congregationalist minister, was pastor of Fifth Avenue Presbyterian Church in New York, then succeeded G. Campbell Morgan at Westminster Chapel in London.

[4] Stephen Neill, *On the Ministry* (n.p., n.d.), 107–8. Bishop Azariah (1874–1945) was the first Indian bishop in the Anglican church. He founded the Missionary Society of Tinnevelly in 1903. He co-founded the National Missionary Society for the evangelization of India.

Essential Qualities of Leadership

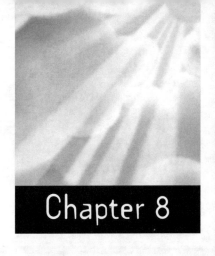

Now the overseer must be above reproach, the husband of but one wife, temper-ate, self-controlled, respectable, hospitable, able to teach, not given to drunken-ness, not violent but gentle, not quarrelsome, not a lover of money. He must manage his own family well and see that his children obey him with proper respect. (If anyone does not know how to manage his own family, how can he take care of God's church?) He must not be a recent convert, or he may become conceited, and fall under the same judgment as the devil. He must also have a good reputation with outsiders, so that he will not fall into disgrace and into the devil's trap.

— 1 Timothy 3:2-7

Discipline
Patience
Weekend Warrior

Discipline
Vision
Wisdom
Decision
Courage
Humility

Jesus trained His disciples superbly for their future roles. He taught by example and by precept; His teaching was done "on the way." Jesus did not ask the Twelve to sit down and take notes in a formal classroom. Jesus' classrooms were the highways of life; His principles and values came across in the midst of daily experience. Jesus placed disciples into internships (Luke 10:17-24) that enabled them to learn through failure and success (Mark 9:14-29). He delegated authority and responsibility to them as they were able to bear it. The disciples grew to understand faith for daily needs and developed their ability to assume authority and responsibility. Jesus' wonderful teaching in John 13-16 was their graduation address.

God prepares leaders with a specific place and task in mind. Training methods are adapted to the mission, and natural and spiritual gifts are given with clear purpose. An example is Paul, who never could have accomplished so much without directed training and divine endowment.

How has God prepared you for the leadership role you now have?

Similarly, God prepared Adoniram Judson to become a missionary pioneer in Burma by giving to this remarkable leader qualities necessary for launching the gospel in the Indian subcontinent—self-reliance balanced by humility, energy restrained by prudence, self-forgetfulness, courage, and a passion for souls.

Martin Luther has been described as a man easy to approach, without personal vanity, and so plain in his tastes that people wondered how he could sustain life with so little. He had common sense, a playful humor, eager laughter, sincerity, and honesty. Added to those qualities were his courage, conviction, and passion for Christ. It is no wonder that he inspired loyalty that had the strength of steel.[1]

Professor G. Warneck described Hudson Taylor, the missionary pioneer to China: "A man full of faith and the Holy Ghost, of entire surrender to God and His call, of great self-denial, heartfelt compassion, rare power in prayer, marvelous organizing faculty, indefatigable perseverance, and of astounding influence with men, and withal of childlike simplicity himself."[2]

God gave these leaders gifts and talents that fit the mission to which they were called. What raised these men above their fellows was the degree to which they developed those gifts through devotion and discipline.

Discipline

Without this essential quality, all other gifts remain as dwarfs: they cannot grow. So discipline appears first on our list. Before we can conquer the world, we must first conquer the self.

A leader is a person who has learned to obey a discipline imposed from without, and has then taken on a more rigorous discipline from within. Those who rebel against authority and scorn self-discipline—who shirk the rigors and turn from the sacrifices—do not qualify to lead. Many who drop out of ministry are sufficiently gifted, but have large areas of life floating free from the Holy Spirit's control. Lazy and disorganized people never rise to true leadership.

Many who aspire to leadership fail because they have never learned to follow. They are like boys playing war in the street, but all is quiet. When you ask, "Is there a truce?" they respond, "No, we are all generals. No one will obey the command to charge."

Donald Barnhouse noted with interest that the average age of the 40,000 people listed in *Who's Who in America*—the people who run the country—was under 28. Discipline in early life, which is prepared to make sacrifices in order to gain adequate preparation for the life-task, paves the way for high achievement.[3]

A great statesman made a speech that turned the tide of national affairs. "May I ask how long you spent preparing that speech?" asked an admirer.

"All my life," he replied.

What do you learn about leadership and accomplishments from the above anecdote?

The young man of leadership caliber will work while others waste time, study while others snooze, pray while others daydream. Slothful habits are overcome, whether in thought, deed, or dress. The emerging leader eats right, stands tall, and prepares himself to wage a good warfare. He will without reluctance undertake the unpleasant task that others avoid or the hidden duty that others evade because it wins no public applause. As the Spirit fills his life, he learns not to shrink from difficult situations or retreat from hard-edged people. He will kindly and courageously administer rebuke when that is called for, or he will exercise the necessary discipline when the interests of the Lord's work demands it. He will gain the ability to rebuke another with courage and measured forcefulness. He will not procrastinate, but will prefer to dispatch with the hardest tasks first. His prayer will be:

> God, harden me against myself,
> The coward with pathetic voice
> Who craves for ease and rest and joy.
> Myself, arch-traitor to myself,
> My hollowest friend,
> My deadliest foe,
> My clog, whatever road I go.[4]

Few men were more faithful and courageous in giving loving rebuke or speaking frankly to people than Fred Mitchell, British director of the China Inland Mission and chairman of the English Keswick Convention. Sensitive and affectionate, he did not turn from the unpleasant interview. He always spoke in love, after much prayer. But his words did not always fall on receptive ears. He confided how much he had suffered when his faithfulness to God's work led to the loss of a friend. As he reached older age, Fred spent even more time praying before speaking. Often when he needed to deal with a matter of discipline or cut across the desires of others, he would write a letter, then keep it for several days. Sometimes on rereading it, he was assured it was right to send it, and it would be mailed. Sometimes he destroyed the draft and wrote another.[5]

When the founder of the World Dominion Movement, Thomas Cochrane, was interviewed for the mission field, he faced this question: "To what position of the field do you feel yourself specially called?" He answered, "I only know I should wish it to be the hardest you could offer me"—the reply of a disciplined person.

Lytton Strachey described Florence Nightingale:

> It was not by gentle sweetness and womanly self-abnegation that she brought order out of chaos in the Scutari hospitals, that from her own resources she had clothed the British Army, that she had spread her dominion over the serried and reluctant powers of the official world; it was by strict method, by *stern discipline*, by rigid attention to detail, by ceaseless labour, by the fixed determination of an indomitable will. Beneath her cool and calm demeanour, there lurked fierce and passionate fires.[6]

Samuel Chadwick, the great Methodist preacher and principal of Cliff College, made an immense impact on his generation. He rose at six each morning and took a cold bath, summer and winter. His study light was seldom out before two in the morning. That rigorous lifestyle was the outward expression of his intense inner discipline.[7]

Throughout his life, George Whitefield rose at four in the morning and retired each night at ten. When that hour struck, he would rise from his seat, no matter who his visitors or what the conversation, and say good-naturedly to his friends, "Come, gentleman, it is time for all good folks to be at home."[8]

Barclay Buxton of Japan would urge Christians to lead disciplined lives whether they were in business or evangelistic work. This included discipline in Bible study and prayer, in tithing their money, in use of their time, in keeping healthy by proper food and sleep and exercise. It included the rigor of disci-plined fellowship among Christians who differed from one another in many ways. [These] disciplines of his life, and his urgings for others, came because of experience.[9]

These pieces of personal biography illustrate the meaning of an unknown poet:

> The heights by great men reached and kept
> Were not attained by sudden flight;
> But they, while their companions slept,
> Were toiling upward in the night.

If a leader demonstrates strong self-discipline, others will sense that and usually cooperate with the expectations placed on them.

There is another element in discipline that receives too little attention. We must be willing to receive from others as well as give to others. Some sacrificial souls delight in sacrificing themselves but are unwilling to allow others to reci-procate. They do not want to feel obligated to others. But leadership requires openness to others. To neglect receiving kindness and help is to isolate oneself, to rob others of opportunity, and to deprive oneself of sustenance.

Do you have difficulty receiving from others? Describe what can result from being unwilling to receive from others.

Bishop Westcott admitted at the end of his life to one great mistake. He had always helped others, but just as rigorously he had resisted others' serving him. As a result, his life had an empty spot where sweet friendship and human care might have been.[10]

Vision

Those who have most powerfully and permanently influenced their generation have been "seers"—people who have seen more and farther than others—

persons of faith, for faith is vision. Moses, one of the great leaders of all history, "endured as seeing him who is invisible." His faith imparted vision. Elijah's servant saw vividly the vast encircling army, but Elijah saw the hosts of heaven. His faith imparted vision.

Powhatten James wrote:

> The man of God must have insight into things spiritual. He must be able to see the mountains filled with the horses and chariots of fire; he must be able to interpret that which is written by the finger of God upon the walls of conscience; he must be able to translate the signs of the times into terms of their spiritual meaning; he must be able to draw aside, now and then, the curtain of things material and let mortals glimpse the spiritual glories which crown the mercy seat of God. The man of God must declare the pattern that was shown him on the mount; he must utter the vision granted to him upon the isle of revelation. . . . None of these things can he do without spiritual insight.[11]

How can lack of vision hold back Christian ministry?

Charles Cowman, founder of the Oriental Missionary Society, was "a man of vision. Throughout his life he seemed to see what the crowd did not see, and to see wider and fuller than many of his own day. He was a man of far horizons."[12]

Vision involves foresight as well as insight. President McKinley's reputation for greatness rested in part on his ability to put an ear to the ground and listen for things coming. He turned his listening into vision; he saw what lay ahead. A leader must be able to see the end results of the policies and methods he or she advocates. Responsible leadership always looks ahead to see how policies will affect future generations.

The great missionary pioneers were people of vision. Carey saw the whole globe while fellow preachers defined the world at their parish borders. Henry Martyn saw India, Persia, and Arabia—the Muslim world—while the church at home squabbled over petty theological disagreements. People said of A. B. Simpson: "His life-work seemed to be to push on alone, where his fellows had seen nothing to explore."

A senior colleague once told Douglas Thornton of Egypt: "Thornton, you are different from anyone else I know. You are always looking at the end of things. Most people, myself included, find it better to do the next thing." Thornton's answer: "I find that the constant inspiration gained by looking at the goal is the chief thing that helps me to persevere."[13] An ideal, a vision, was absolutely necessary to him. He could not work without it. And that explained the largeness of his views and the magnitude of his schemes.

Eyes that look are common; eyes that see are rare. The Pharisees *looked* at Peter and saw only an unschooled fisherman—not worth a second look. Jesus *saw* Peter as a prophet and preacher, saint and leader who helped turn the world upside down.

Vision includes optimism and hope. The pessimist sees difficulty in every opportunity. The optimist sees opportunity in every difficulty. The pessimist tends to hold back people of vision from pushing ahead. Caution has its role to play. The cautious person helps the optimistic leader to be realistic. We all live in a real world of limitation and inertia. Cautious Christians draw valuable lessons from history and tradition, but are in danger of being chained to the past. The person who sees the difficulties so clearly that he does not discern the possibilities cannot inspire a vision in others.

Robert Browning described the courageous optimist:

> One who has never turned his back,
> But marched breast-forward,
> Never doubting clouds would break,
> Never dreamed, though right were worsted,
> Wrong would triumph.

Vision leads to venture, and history is on the side of venturesome faith. The person of vision takes fresh steps of faith across gullies and chasms, not "playing it safe" but neither taking foolish risks.

Describe some elements needed for spiritual vision.

Concerning Archbishop Mowll it is written:

> It was a mark of his greatness that he was never behind his age, or too far ahead. He was up at the front, and far enough in advance to lead the march. He was always catching sight of new horizons. He still had a receptive mind for new ideas at an age when many were inclined to let things take their course.[14]

Leaders take lessons from the past, but never sacrifice the future for the sake of mere continuity. People of vision gauge decisions on the future; the story of the past cannot be rewritten.

> A vision without a task makes a visionary.
> A task without a vision is drudgery.
> A vision with a task makes a missionary.[15]

Wisdom

"Wisdom is the faculty of making the use of knowledge, a combination of discernment, judgment, sagacity, and similar powers. . . . In Scripture, right judgment concerning spiritual and moral truth" (Webster).

If knowledge is the accumulation of facts, and intelligence the development of reason, wisdom is heavenly discernment. It is insight into the heart of things. Wisdom involves knowing God and the subtleties of the human heart. More than knowledge, it is the right application of knowledge in moral and spiritual matters, in handling dilemmas, in negotiating complex relationships. "Wisdom is nine-tenths a matter of being wise in time," said Theodore Roosevelt. Most of us are "too often wise after the event."[16]

Wisdom gives a leader balance and helps to avoid eccentricity and extravagance. If knowledge comes by study, wisdom comes by Holy Spirit filling. Then a leader can apply knowledge correctly. "Full of wisdom" was one of the requirements for even subordinate leaders in the early church (Acts 6:3).

Complete these statements:
    A. Wisdom is heavenly _____.

    B. Wisdom involves _____ God.

    C. Wisdom comes by the filling of the _____ _____.

> Knowledge and wisdom, far from being one,
> Have ofttimes no connection. Knowledge dwells
> In heads replete with thoughts of other men:
> Wisdom, in minds attentive to their own.
> Knowledge is proud that he has learned so much,
> Wisdom is humble, that he knows no more.
>
> —Author unknown

D. E. Hoste knew the importance of wisdom for leaders:

> When a man, in virtue of an official position, demands obedience of another, irrespective of the latter's reason and conscience, this is the spirit of tyranny. When on the other hand, by the exercise of tact and sympathy; by prayer, spiritual power and sound wisdom one is able to influence and enlighten another, so that he through the medium of his own reason and conscience is led to alter one course and adopt another, that is true spiritual leadership.[17]

Paul's prayer for the Christians at Colossae should always be on our lips: That God "fill you with the knowledge of his will through all spiritual wisdom and understanding" (Col. 1:9).

Explain the difference in meanings of these pairs of words:
    A. Knowledge/Wisdom

    is   is
    acquired   given

Decision

When all the facts are in, swift and clear decision is the mark of a true leader. A visionary may see, but a leader must decide. An impulsive person may be quick to declare a preference; but a leader must weigh evidence and make his decision on sound premises.

Once sure of the will of God, a spiritual leader springs into action, without regard to consequences. Pursuing the goal, the leader never looks back or calculates escape strategies if plans turn sour. Neither does a true leader cast blame for failure on subordinates.

Abraham showed swift and clear decisiveness during the crisis at Sodom and the rescue of Lot (Gen. 14). In his relations with Lot, Abraham showed both the active and passive sides of spirituality. In his unselfish yielding of his right to the choice of pasturelands (Gen. 13), Abraham had displayed the passive graces of godliness. But when Lot was captured during the battle at Sodom in Genesis 14, Abraham displayed immediate decision and initiative. With great bravery he pursued the enemy and gained a victory over superior numbers. This is true faith.

Moses became the leader of Israel when he abandoned Egypt's power and privilege and identified with the Hebrew slaves and their suffering (Heb. 11:24-27). These were momentous decisions. This is faith.

Paul's first question after his dramatic conversion was "What shall I do, Lord?" (Acts 22:10). Without hesitation Paul acted on his new knowledge of Christ's deity. To be granted light was to follow it. To see duty was to do it.

The catalog of saints in Hebrews 11 is a study of vision and decision. They saw the vision, counted the cost, made their decisions, and went into action. The same movement is evident in the lives of great missionary leaders. Carey saw the vision in Kettering and made his decision for India, though the difficulties of getting there loomed as high as heaven itself. Livingstone saw the vision in Dumbarton, made his decision, overcame all obstacles, and proceeded to Africa.[18] Circumstances cannot frustrate such people, or difficulties deter them.

"The catalog of saints in Hebrews 11 is a study of vision and decision." They:

_____ the vision, _____ the cost,

_____ their decisions, and _____ into action.

Has there been a decisive time in your ministry when you followed the example of the saints in Hebrews 11? Summarize the event:

1. Seeing the vision:

2. Counting the cost:

3. Making the decision:

4. Going into action:

The spiritual leader will not procrastinate when faced with a decision, neither will he vacillate after making it. A sincere but faulty decision is worse than weak-willed "trial balloons" or indecisive overtures. To postpone decision is really to decide for the status quo. In most decisions the key element is not so much knowing what to do, but in living with the results.

Charles Cowman had the reputation of being a man of purpose. His eyes were fixed on one great object. With him, a vision was the first step in an action plan. The moment he sensed a possibility, he was uneasy until achievement was underway.

A young man beginning his work with the Coast Guard was called with his crew to try a desperate rescue in a great storm. Frightened, rain and wind pounding his face, the man cried to his captain, "We will never get back!" The captain replied, "We don't have to come back, but we must go out."

Courage

Leaders require courage of the highest order—always moral courage and often physical courage as well. Courage is that quality of mind which enables people to encounter danger or difficulty firmly, without fear or discouragement.

Paul admitted to knowing fear, but it never stopped him. "I came to you in weakness and fear, and with much trembling," he reported in 1 Corinthians 2:3, but the verb is *came*. He did not stay home out of fear for the journey.

What lesson about courage do you learn from Paul in 1 Corinthians 2:3?

In 2 Corinthians 7:5, Paul confesses that he experienced "conflicts on the out-side, fears within." He did not court danger, but he never let it keep him from the Master's work.

Martin Luther was among the most fearless men who ever lived.[19] When he set out on his journey to Worms to face the questions and the controversies his teaching had created, he said, "You can expect from me everything save fear or recantation. I shall not flee, much less recant." His friends warned of the dangers; some begged him not to go. But Luther would not hear of it. "Not go to Worms!" he said. "I shall go to Worms though there were as many devils as tiles on the roofs."[20]

When Luther appeared there before the court of Emperor Charles V, he was shown a stack of his writings and called upon to recant. Luther replied, "Unless

I can be instructed and convinced with evidence from the Holy Scriptures or with open, clear, and distinct grounds of reasoning, then I cannot and will not recant, because it is neither safe nor wise to act against conscience."

Then he likely added: "Here I stand. I can do no other. God help me! Amen."

A few days before his death Luther recalled that day. "I was afraid of nothing: God can make one so desperately bold."

According to Martin Luther, what is the key to courage?

_____

Not everyone is courageous by nature. Some people are more naturally timid than Luther. But whether we are bold or reticent, God calls leaders to be of good courage and not to capitulate to fear. Such a call to courage would be rather pointless if nobody feared anything. Because fear is a real part of life, God gives us the Holy Spirit, who fills us with power. But we must let that power do its work, and not fear.

Consider these two contrasting statements: "With the doors locked for fear of the Jews" (John 20:19), and, "When they saw the courage of Peter and John" (Acts 4:13). These statements describe the same disciples and the same opposition. What happened between the first incident and the second? The difference is the Holy Spirit. "All of them were filled with the Holy Spirit" (Acts 2:4). And when the Holy Spirit is given control of the personality, He gives not "a spirit of timidity, but a spirit of power" (2 Tim. 1:7).

Courageous leaders face unpleasant and even devastating situations with equanimity, then act firmly to bring good from trouble, even if their action is unpopular. Leadership always faces natural human inertia and opposition. But courage follows through with a task until it is done.

People expect leaders to be calm and courageous during a crisis. While others lose their heads, leaders stay the course. Leaders strengthen followers in the middle of discouraging setbacks and shattering reverses.

Facing the ruthless armies of Sennacherib, Hezekiah made his military preparations and then set about strengthening the morale of his people. "Be strong and courageous," he told them. "Do not be afraid or discouraged because of the king of Assyria and the vast army with him, for there is a greater power with us than with him. . . . With him is only the arm of flesh, but with us is the LORD our God to help us and to fight our battles." And then the Scriptures report that "the people gained confidence from what Hezekiah the king of Judah said" (2 Chron. 32:7-8). Here is leadership, active and strong.

Humility

Humility is the hallmark of the spiritual leader. Christ told His disciples to turn away from the pompous attitudes of the oriental despots, and instead take on the lowly bearing of the servant (Matt. 20:25-27). As in ancient days, so today humility is least admired in political and business circles. But no bother! The spiritual leader will choose the hidden path of sacrificial service and approval of the Lord over the flamboyant self-advertising of the world.

We often regard John the Baptist as great because of his burning eloquence and blistering denunciation of the evils of his day. His words pierced and exposed the hearts of many a petty ruler. But his real greatness was revealed in one infinitely wise affirmation: "He must become greater; I must become less" (John 3:30). Here John's spiritual stature rings clear and strong.

A leader's humility should grow with the passing of years, like other attitudes and qualities. Notice Paul's advance in the grace of humility. Early in his ministry, he acknowledged: "I am the least of the apostles and do not even deserve to be called an apostle" (1 Cor. 15:9). Later he volunteered: "I am less than the least of all God's people" (Eph. 3:8). Toward the end of his life he spoke of the mercies of Christ and his own sense of place: "Christ Jesus came into the world to save sinners—of whom I am the worst" (1 Tim. 1:15).

William Law writes in his devotional classic *Serious Call*:

> Let every day be a day of humility; condescend to all the weaknesses and infirmities of your fellow-creatures, cover their frailties, love their excellencies, encourage their virtues, relieve their wants, rejoice in their prosperities, compassionate their distress, receive their friendship, overlook their unkindness, forgive their malice, be a servant of servants, and condescend to do the lowliest offices of the lowest of mankind.[21]

On one occasion when Samuel Brengle was introduced as "the great Doctor Brengle," he noted in his diary:

> If I appear great in their eyes, the Lord is most graciously helping me to see how absolutely nothing I am without Him, and helping me to keep little in my own eyes. He does use me. But I am so concerned that He uses me and that it is not of me the work is done. The axe cannot boast of the trees it has cut down. It could do nothing but for the woodsman. He made it, he sharpened it, and he used it. The moment he throws it aside; it becomes only old iron. O that I may never lose sight of this.[22]

The spiritual leader of today is the one who gladly works as an assistant and associate, humbly helping another achieve great things. Robert Morrison of China wrote: "The great fault, I think, in our missions is that no one likes to be second."[23]

> **Explain in your own words why the following quote**
> **from Samuel Brengle is relevant to spiritual leadership.**
> **"The axe cannot boast of the trees it has cut down.**
> **It could do nothing but for the woodsman."**

Integrity and Sincerity

Paul spoke of his failures and successes with an openness few of us are prepared to copy. Even before his conversion he served God sincerely (2 Tim. 1:3) and with great personal integrity. Later he wrote: "In Christ we speak before God with sincerity" (2 Cor. 2:17).

These two qualities of leadership were part of God's law for the Israelites (Deut. 18:13). God wants His people to show a transparent character, open and innocent of guile.

A prominent businessman once replied to a question: "If I had to name the one most important quality of a top manager, I would say, 'Personal integrity.'" Surely the spiritual leader must be sincere in promise, faithful in discharge of duty, upright in finances, loyal in service, and honest in speech.

---

[1] James Burns, *Revivals, Their Laws and Leaders* (London: Hodder & Stoughton, 1909), 182. Martin Luther (1483–1546) is generally credited for beginning the Protestant Reformation when he nailed "95 Theses" (statements outlining his understanding of the Scriptures contrasted to church teachings) on the church door at Wittenberg, Germany, in October 1517. Adoniram Judson (1788–1850), mentioned earlier, is widely known as a pioneer missionary to Burma.

[2] Gustav Warneck (1834–1910) is generally recognized as the founder of the field of study called missiology.

[3] Donald Grey Barnhouse (1895–1960) worked in Belgium and France before taking the pastorate of Tenth Presbyterian Church in Philadelphia. He edited *Revelation*, later *Eternity* magazine, and wrote extensively.

[4] Used by permission of Christian Literature Crusade, Fort Washington, Pennsylvania. Amy Wilson Carmichael (1867–1951), missionary to India, founded the Dohnavur Fellowship to help neglected and abused children. She served 56 years without a furlough and wrote 35 books.

[5] Phyllis Thompson, *Climbing on Track* (London: China Inland Mission, 1954), 116.

[6] Florence Nightingale (1820–1910), heroine of the Crimean War and founder of modern nursing, felt called to serve God at age 17. Adulation flowed from her work in Scutari, Turkey, on behalf of British troops. She became a recluse, however, for the last four decades of her life.

[7] N. G. Dunning, *Samuel Chadwick* (London: Hodder & Stoughton, 1934), 15. Chadwick lived from 1860–1932.

[8] J. R. Andrews, *George Whitefield* (London: Morgan & Scott, 1915), 410–11. Barclay Buxton (1860–1946) mentioned immediately after this citation, was a missionary to Japan for 46 years.

[9] *World Vision,* January 1966, 5.

[10] Brooke Foss Westcott (1825–1901) worked for 28 years with Fenton Hort on *The New Testament in the Original Greek* (1881). His Bible commentaries are still read.

[11] Powhatten James, *George W. Truett* (Nashville: Broadman, 1953), 266. Truett lived from 1867 to 1944.

[12] Lettie B. Cowman, *Charles E. Cowman* (Los Angeles: Oriental Missionary Society, 1928), 259. Charles Cowman founded the Oriental Missionary Society, now known as OMS International, in 1901.

Lettie Cowman wrote *Streams in the Desert,* one of the most-read devotional books of all time. William McKinley (1843–1901), mentioned immediately after this citation, was the 25th president of the United States.

[13] W. H. T. Gairdner, *Douglas M. Thornton* (London: Hodder & Stoughton, n.d.), 80. Thornton (1873–1907) was educational secretary for the Student Volunteer Missionary Union. Henry Martyn (1781–1812), mentioned in the previous paragraph, was inspired to a life in missions after reading the diary of David Brainerd. He served as chaplain to the East India Company in Bengal, and translated the New Testament into Hindustani. Albert Benjamin Simpson (1844–1915) founded the Evangelical Missionary Alliance, later the Christian and Missionary Alliance, and wrote more than 70 books.

[14] Marcus Lane, *Archbishop Mowll* (London: Hodder & Stoughton, 1960), 202. Howard West Kilvington Mowll (1890–1958) served as an Anglican bishop in Canada, China, and Sydney (Australia).

[15] Dunning, 20.

[16] Theodore Roosevelt, in B. Matthews, *John R. Mott* (London: S.C.M. Press, 1934), 355. Roosevelt (1858–1919) was the 26th president of the United States.

[17] Phyllis Thompson, *D. E. Hoste* (London: China Inland Mission, n.d.), 155.

[18] David Livingstone (1813–1873), while a young boy, taught himself Greek, theology, and medicine. In 1840 he went to Africa under the London Missionary Society. When he was found by *New York Herald* journalist Henry Stanley in 1871, Stanley greeted Livingstone with the oft-quoted words: "Doctor Livingstone, I presume."

[19] Burns, 181–82.

[20] Ibid., 167–68. Luther's precise words at the Diet of Worms are the subject of historians' debates. Sanders's original text quotes from Burns. More recent historical data was used for the quotation in this edition. See James M. Kittelson, "The Accidental Revolutionary," in *Christian History*, Issue 34, 16. Quotations preceding Worms and near the time of Luther's death are reported as they appear in Burns.

[21] William Law (1686–1761) was an evangelical devotional writer and mystic.

[22] C. W. Hall, *Samuel Logan Brengle* (New York: Salvation Army, 1933), 275.

[23] Robert Morrison (1782–1834) was an interpreter for the East India Company in Canton. He translated the Bible into Cantonese, and labored for 27 years in China for about a dozen converts.

More Essential Qualities of Leadership

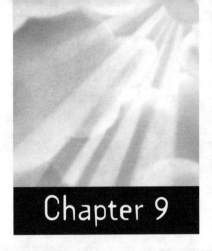

Deacons, likewise, are to be men worthy of respect, sincere, not indulging in much wine, and not pursuing dishonest gain. They must keep hold of the deep truths of the faith with a clear conscience. They must first be tested; and then if there is nothing against them, let them serve as deacons.

—1 Timothy 3:8-10

Humor

Our sense of humor is a gift from God which should be controlled as well as cultivated. Clean, wholesome humor will relax tension and relieve difficult situations. Leaders can use it to displace tension with a sense of the normal.

Samuel Johnson advised that people should spend part of each day laughing. Archbishop Whately, the great apologist, wrote: "We ought not only to cultivate the cornfield of the mind but the pleasure grounds also." Agnes Strickland claimed that "next to virtue, the fun in this world is what we can least spare."[1]

Criticized for including humor in a sermon, Charles Spurgeon, eyes twinkling, said: "If only you knew how much I hold back, you would commend me." Later writing on the subject, he said: "There are things in these sermons that may produce smiles, but what of them? The preacher is not quite sure about a smile being a sin, and at any rate he thinks it less a crime to cause a momentary laughter than a half-hour of profound slumber."

Helmut Thielecke wrote:

> Should we not see that lines of laughter about the eyes are just as much marks of faith as are the lines of care and seriousness? Is it only earnestness that is baptized? Is laughter pagan? . . . A church is in a bad way when it banishes laughter from the sanctuary and leaves it to the cabaret, the nightclub and the toastmasters.[2]

Humor is a great asset and an invaluable lubricant in missionary life. Indeed it is a most serious deficiency if a missionary lacks a sense of humor. A Swede was urged by friends to give up the idea of returning to India as a missionary because it was so hot there. "Man," he was urged, "it is one hundred twenty degrees in the shade!"

"Vell," said the Swede in noble contempt, "ve don't always have to stay in the shade, do ve?"

A. E. Norrish, a missionary to India, testified:

> I have never met leadership without a sense of humor; this ability to stand outside oneself and one's circumstances, to see things in perspective and laugh. It is a great safety valve! You will never lead others far without the joy of the Lord and its concomitant, a sense of humor.[3]

Douglas Thornton was often more amusing than he tried to be. He had a delightful way of mixing up two kindred proverbs or idioms. Once he told his companions that he always had two strings up his sleeve. They then asked him if he also had another card to his bow. Such things enliven heavy committee meetings and create wholesome laughter.

After a half century of ministry, F. J. Hallett claimed that in the actual work of a parish, the most successful leader is the one who possesses a keen sense of humor combined with a clear sense of God's grace.

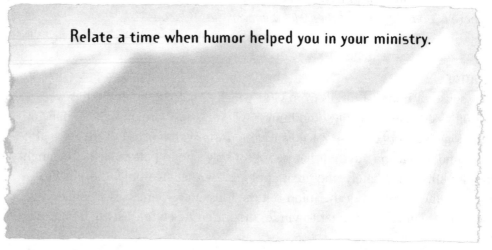

Relate a time when humor helped you in your ministry.

Humor lends pungency, originality, and eloquence to sermons. Of one great preacher it was said that he used humor as a condiment and a stimulant. At times paroxysms of laugher would rock his audience—never about sacred matters. Following the joke, he would quickly swing to the sublime. His humor never fell into frivolity.

A good test of the appropriateness of a joke is whether the humor controls us or we control it. About Kenneth Strachan, general director of the Latin American Mission, it was said: "He had a keen sense of humor, but he had a sense of the fitness of things. He knew the place for a joke and his humor was controlled."[4]

Anger

Can this be right? An angry leader? Indeed, Jesus had this quality; and when we use it rightly, we follow Him. In Mark 3:5, Jesus looked "at them in anger."

Holy anger is the counterpart to love. Both are part of the nature of God. Jesus' love for the man with the withered hand aroused His anger against those who would deny him healing. Jesus' love for God's house made Him angry at the sellers and buyers who had turned the temple into a "den of robbers" (Matt. 21:13).

Great leaders—people who turn the tide and change the direction of events—have been angry at injustice and abuse that dishonors God and enslaves the weak. Wilberforce moved heaven and earth to emancipate slaves in England and eliminate the slave trade—and he was angry!

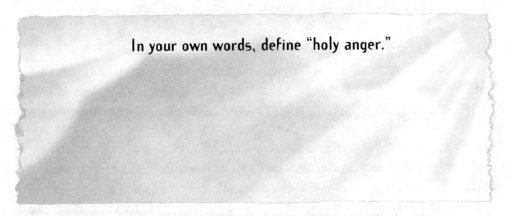

In your own words, define "holy anger."

F. W. Robertson described his sense of anger on one special occasion: "My blood was at the moment running fire, and I remembered that once in my life I had felt a terrible might; I knew and rejoiced to know that I was inflicting the sentence of a coward's and a liar's hell."[5]

Martin Luther claimed that he "never did anything well until his wrath was excited, and then he could do anything well."

But holy anger is open to abuse. Many who feel it allow anger to become their downfall. Bishop Butler teaches six conditions that make anger sinful:

- When, to favor a resentment or feud, we imagine an injury done to us
- When an injury done to us becomes, in our minds, greater than it really is
- When, without real injury, we feel resentment on account of pain or inconvenience
- When indignation rises too high and overwhelms our ability to restrain
- When we gratify resentments by causing pain or harm out of revenge
- When we are so perplexed and angry at sin in our own lives that we readily project anger at the sin we find in others.[6]

Paul argues for holy anger when he repeats the advice of Psalm 4:4: "In your anger do not sin" (Eph. 4:26).

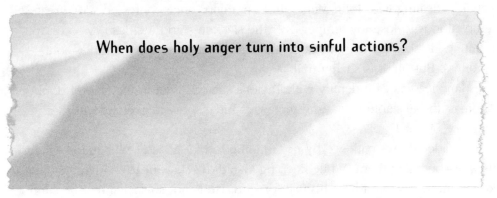

When does holy anger turn into sinful actions?

This anger is not selfish and does not center on the pain you currently feel. To be free of sin such anger must be zealous for truth and purity, with the glory of God its chief objective.

Thou to wax fierce
In the cause of the Lord!
Anger and zeal
And the joy of the brave,
Who bade thee to feel,
Sin's slave?
—Author unknown

Patience

Spiritual leaders need a healthy endowment of patience. Chrysostom called patience the queen of virtues. Often we think of patience in passive terms, as if the patient person is utterly submissive and half asleep. But this version of patience needs a biblical corrective. Barclay teaches from 2 Peter 1:6 (where the King James Version uses the term *patience*):

> The word never means the spirit which sits with folded hands and simply bears things. It is victorious endurance [and] constancy under trial. It is Christian steadfastness, the brave and courageous acceptance of everything life can do to us, and the transmuting of even the worst into another step on the upward way. It is the courageous and triumphant ability to bear things, which enables a man to pass breaking point and not to break, and always to greet the unseen with a cheer.[7]

Explain how patience is an active, not passive, quality of a leader.

Patience meets its most difficult test in personal relationships. Paul lost his patience dealing with John Mark. Hudson Taylor once confessed: "My greatest temptation is to lose my temper over the slackness and inefficiency so disappointing in those on whom I depend. It is no use to lose my temper—only kindness. But oh, it is such a trial."[8]

Many leaders can identify with Taylor's struggle. But in the face of doubting Thomas, the unstable Peter, and traitorous Judas, how marvelous was the patience of our Lord!

A leader shows patience by not running too far ahead of his followers and thus discouraging them. While keeping ahead, he stays near enough for them to keep him in sight and hear his call forward. He is not so strong that he cannot show a strengthening sympathy for the weakness of his fellows. "We who are strong ought to bear with the failings of the weak," Paul wrote in Romans 15:1.

The person who is impatient with weakness will be defective in his leadership. The evidence of our strength lies not in the distance that separates us from other runners, but in our closure with them, our slower pace for their sakes, our helping them pick it up and cross the line.

> **Why is it important for a leader to be patient and not go too far ahead of his followers?**
>
> **Is this a problem area for you?**
>
> **If so, what steps can you take to close the gap?**

Ernest Gordon described his father, A. J. Gordon, with these words: "Criticism and opposition he endured without recrimination."[9]

When we lead by persuasion rather than command, patience is essential. Leaders rightly cultivate the art of persuasion that allows maximum individual decision making and ownership of a plan. Often, a leader's plan of action must wait for collegial support—ever patient—until the team is ready. D. E. Hoste remembered a great leader:

> I shall never forget the impression made upon me by Hudson Taylor in connection with these affairs. Again and again he was obliged either to greatly modify or lay aside projects which were sound and helpful but met with determined opposition. . . . Later, in answer to patience continuance in prayer, many of [these] projects were [put into] effect.[10]

Friendship

You can measure leaders by the number and quality of their friends. Judged by that measuring rod, Paul had a genius for friendship. He was essentially a gregarious man. His relationship with Timothy was a model of friendship between generations; Paul and Luke are a model between contemporaries.

A. B. Simpson earned this sterling tribute: "The crowning glory of his leadership was that he was a friend of man. He loved the man next to him and he loved mankind."[11] David's leadership sprang from his genius at gathering around him men of renown who were ready to die for him. So fully did he capture their affection and allegiance that a whispered wish was to them as a command (2 Sam. 23:15-16). They were prepared to die for him because they knew David was fully ready to die for them.

The apostle Paul similarly had loyal friends. "No man in the New Testament made fiercer enemies than Paul, but few men in the world had better friends. They clustered around him so thickly that we are apt to lose their personality in their devotion."[12] Yes, Paul led his friends into all sorts of risks for Christ's sake; but they followed him cheerfully, confident of his love for them. Paul's letters glow with warm appreciation and personal affection for his fellows.

Leaders must draw the best out of people, and friendship does that far better than prolonged argument or mere logic. John R. Mott counseled leaders to "rule by the heart. When logic and arguments and other forms of persuasion fail, fall back on the heart-genuine friendship."

Robert A. Jaffrey played a major role in opening Vietnam to the gospel. He did so largely because of this quality that all great leaders share. "Nothing can take the place of affection. . . . Intellect will not do. Bible knowledge is not enough. Jaffrey loved people for their own sakes. He was happy in the presence of human beings, whatever their race and colour."[13]

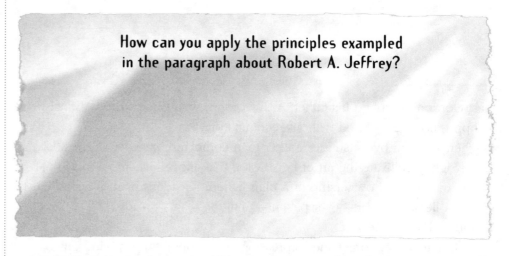

How can you apply the principles exampled in the paragraph about Robert A. Jeffrey?

Few Christian leaders enjoy the reputation won by Charles Spurgeon, the greatest British preacher of the late 19th century. His biographer wrote that "he exercised an absolute authority, not because of sheer willfulness, though he was a willful man, but because of his acknowledged worth. Men bowed to his authority because it was authority backed by united wisdom and affection."

One greater than Spurgeon or David or Paul ruled His followers by friendship and affection. Of Him it was written, "Having loved his own who were in the world, he now showed them the full extent of his love" (John 13:1). Indeed, Peter confessed with broken heart in response to Jesus' enduring affection, "Lord, you know all things; you know that I love you" (John 21:17).

Tact and Diplomacy

The root meaning of *tact* has to do with touching. The tactile sense is the ability to feel through touch. Concerning relationships, tact is the ability to deal with people sensitively, to avoid giving offense, to have a feel for the proper words or responses to a delicate situation.

Diplomacy is the ability to manage delicate situations, especially involving people from different cultures, and certainly from differing opinions.

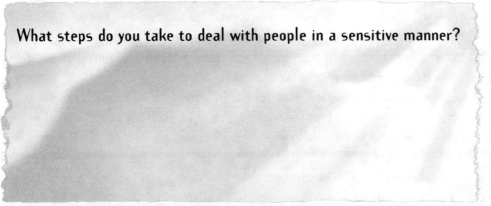

What steps do you take to deal with people in a sensitive manner?

Leaders need to be able to reconcile opposing viewpoints without giving offense or compromising principle. A leader should be able to project into the life and heart and mind of another, then setting aside personal preferences, deal with the other in a fashion that fits the other best. These skills can be learned and developed.

A leader needs the ability to negotiate differences in a way that recognizes mutual rights and intelligence and yet leads to a harmonious solution. Fundamental to this skill is understanding how people feel, how people react.

Joshua used wonderful tact when he divided the promised land among the tribes of Israel. A wrong move would have splintered an already wobbly nation. Joshua had to be both forthright and fair. His tact beamed brightly again when the tribes of Reuben and Gad built their own altar and thus nearly created a civil war. Joshua had wisdom learned in the school of God. His close walk with God gave him the diplomacy to steer a course away from needless bloodshed and toward national healing.

What was Joshua's key to having tact in a difficult situation?

William Carey was unconsciously a diplomat. One of his fellow workers testified: "He has attained the happy art of ruling and overruling others without asserting his authority or others feeling their subjection, and all is done without the least appearance of design on his part."[14]

Inspirational Power

The power of inspiring others to service and sacrifice will mark God's leader. The leader is like a light for others around. Charles Cowman worked hard, but he also possessed the ability to get others to work hard. His zeal and drive and inspiration were infectious.[15]

Pastor Hsi was one of the truly great leaders of his time in China. He, too, possessed this power to an extraordinary degree. A friend commented on Hsi's inspiring presence: "His power in that direction was remarkable; without any effort, apparently, he seemed to sway everybody. Instinctively people followed and trusted him. Then, too, he possessed great power of initiative and energy and enterprise that was extraordinary. One could not be with him without gaining a wholly new ideal of Christian life and service."[16]

Nehemiah had this quality. The people in Jerusalem were utterly disheartened and dispirited when he arrived. In no time he built them into an effective team of workers. Such were his powers that before long we read, "The people had a mind to work."

General Mark Clark, addressing a class of trainees, said of Winston Churchill: "I doubt if any man in history has ever made such grim utterances, yet given his people such a sense of strength, exuberance, even of cheerfulness."[17]

When France fell to the German armies and Britain was left alone in the fight, the British cabinet met in their chambers with a sense of deep gloom. When Churchill entered, he looked around at the disconsolate ministers, then said, "Gentlemen, I find this rather inspiring." Small wonder that he was able to galvanize a nation into effective counterattack.

Executive Ability

However spiritual a leader may be, he cannot translate vision into action without executive ability. It is true that subtle dangers lie in organization, for if it is overzealous it can be an unsatisfactory substitute for the working of the Holy Spirit. But lack of method and failure to organize have spelled doom for many promising ministries.

The King James Version translates Isaiah 30:18: "The LORD is a God of judgment." Here the word *judgment* means method, order, system, or law. So God is methodic and orderly. And God requires of His managers and stewards that "all things be done decently and in order." Bible commentator Sir George Smith writes: "It is a great truth that the Almighty and All-merciful is the All-methodical too. No religion is complete in its creed, or healthy in its influence, which does not insist equally on all these."[18]

Our duty is to reflect the orderliness of God in all we do for Him.

What tools do you use to keep your ministry orderly?

Evangelism is not a matter of organizing people into the kingdom, but neither is evangelistic work justified in ignoring careful planning. We depend on the Spirit leading converts to salvation, but we also plan and act on our plans for the sake of the gospel's reach.

Wesley had a genius for organization that is still evident in the church he founded. Because he was such a gifted executive, his movement was unshaken when death deprived it of his presence and guidance. His judgment of others, his skill in deploying them to the mission's best advantage and to win their loyal submission, amounted to genius and spared the movement from disasters that others experienced.[19]

The Therapy of Listening

To get at the root of problems, a leader must master the art of listening. Too many strong personalities are compulsive talkers. "He won't listen to me," complains a missionary. "He gives the answer before I have had a chance to state the problem."

To many people, sympathetic listening is inefficient—merely waiting until someone else can state a point. But genuine listening seeks to understand another without prejudgment. A problem is often half-solved when it is stated. One missionary casualty moaned: "If only he had listened to me. I needed someone with whom I could share my problem."

Leaders who want to show sensitivity should listen often and long, and talk short and seldom. Many so-called leaders are too busy to listen. True leaders know that time spent listening is well invested.

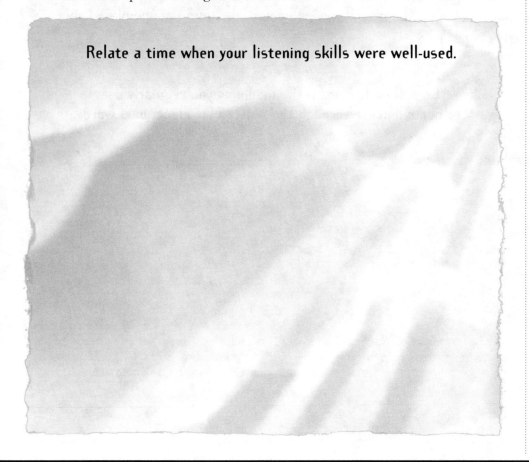

Relate a time when your listening skills were well-used.

A would-be politician approached Justice Oliver Wendell Holmes for advice on how to get elected. Holmes replied: "To be able to listen to others in a sympathetic and understanding manner, is perhaps the most effective mechanism in the world for getting along with people, and tying up their friendship for good."[20]

The Art of Letter Writing

Any position of leadership involves a considerable amount of correspondence, and letters are self-revealing. Take Paul, for example. We know more about his moral integrity, intellectual honesty, and spiritual life from his letters than from any other source. When a difficult situation required his attention, he dipped his pen in tears, not acid. "For I wrote you out of great distress and anguish of heart" (2 Cor. 2:4).

After his strong letter to the erring Corinthians, Paul's tender heart led him to wonder if he had been too severe. "Even if I caused you sorrow by my letter, I do not regret it. Though I did regret it—I see that my letter hurt you, but only for a little while—yet now I am happy . . . because your sorrow led you to repentance" (2 Cor. 7:8-9). The point of his letter was not to win an argument, but to settle a spiritual problem and produce maturity among the Christians there.

Paul's letters abounded in encouragement, were gracious in compliment, and rich in sympathy. Those who received them were always enriched (Phil. 1:27-30). But that did not restrain him from being faithful in correcting faults. "Have I now become your enemy by telling you the truth? . . . How I wish I could be with you now and change my tone, because I am perplexed about you!" (Gal. 4:16, 20).

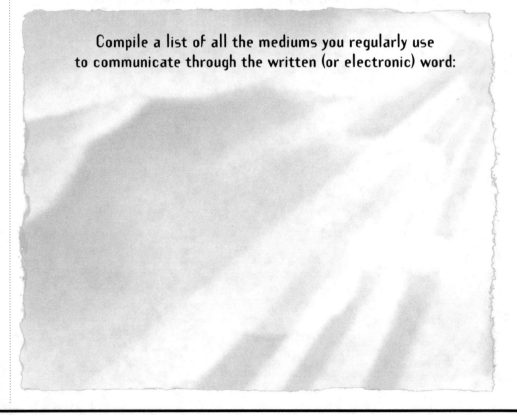

Compile a list of all the mediums you regularly use
to communicate through the written (or electronic) word:

Clear language is important in our letters, but more important is the right spirit. Letters are an unsatisfactory medium of communication. They cannot smile when they are saying something difficult; therefore, additional care should be taken to see that they are warm in tone.

How can you make sure your language and message are clear and warm-spirited?

Letters formed an important part in Paul's program of follow-up. So it was for George Whitefield. It was said of him that after preaching to large crowds, he would work late into the night writing letters of encouragement to new converts.

Review the leadership qualities discussed in chapters 8 and 9.
Follow these instructions:

- Put an X beside the ones you need to develop through devotion and discipline.

- Identify one step you will take immediately to work on this quality.

Discipline

Vision

Wisdom

Decision

Courage

Humility

Integrity

Humor

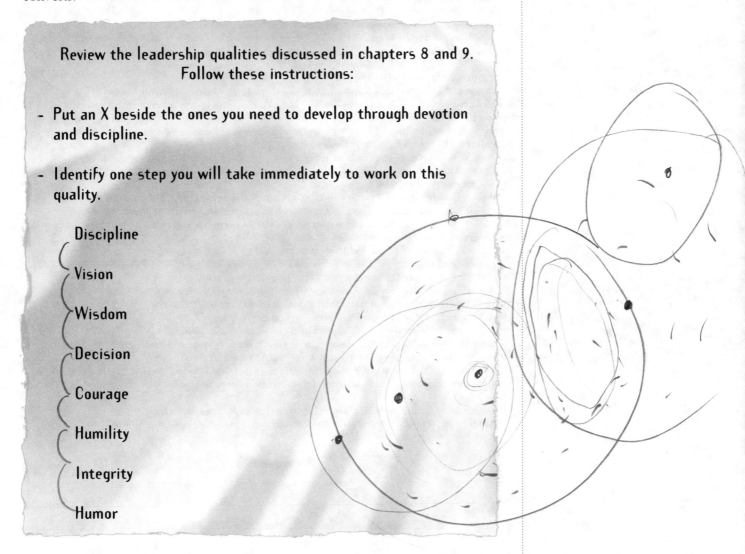

Holy Anger

Patience

Friendship

Tact

Inspirational Power

Executive Abilities

Listening

Written Communication

[1] Quoted in C. W. Hall, *Samuel Logan Brengle* (New York: Salvation Army, 1933), 278. Samuel Johnson (1709–84), mentioned earlier, was an English poet, essayist, and lexicographer. His *Dictionary of the English Language* (1747) was the standard for a century.

[2] Helmut Thielecke, *Encounter with Spurgeon* (Philadelphia: Fortress, 1963), 26. Charles Haddon Spurgeon (1834–92), one of the best-known preachers of the 19th century, was pastor of the Metropolitan Tabernacle in London for 32 years.

[3] A. E. Norrish, *Christian Leadership* (New Delhi: Masihi Sabiyata Sanstha, 1963), 28.

[4] *Latin American Evangelist,* May–June 1965.

[5] Robert E. Speer, *Christ and Life* (New York: Revell, 1901), 103. Frederick William Robertson (1816–53) was ordained in the Church of England in 1840 and made his mark as a preacher among the working poor of Brighton. William Wilberforce (1759–1833), mentioned earlier, was a member of the British parliament whose work, strongly opposed by vested interest, eventually led to laws prohibiting slavery and the slave trade. In 1804 he helped form the British and Foreign Bible Society.

[6] Ibid., 104. The original text has been paraphrased. Joseph Butler (1692–1752), Anglican bishop, is remembered for his book *Analogy of Religion* (1736), probably the best defense of Christian faith to appear in the eighteenth century.

[7] William Barclay, *Letters of Peter and Jude* (Edinburgh: St. Andrews, 1960), 258. John Chrysostom (c. 347–407), mentioned earlier, is one of the early church fathers. He was for 10 years a monastic hermit, then deacon and priest in Antioch, then patriarch of Constantinople. He was exiled for preaching against vice and excess among the clergy and royalty.

[8] J. C. Pollock, *Hudson Taylor and Maria* (London: Hodder & Stoughton, 1962), 35.

[9] Earnest Gordon, *A. J. Gordon* (London: Hodder & Stoughton, 1897), 191.

[10] Phyllis Thompson, *D. E. Hoste* (London: China Inland Mission, n.d.), 158.

[11] A. E. Thompson, *The Life of A. B. Simpson* (Harrisburg: Christian Publications, 1920), 204.

[12] H. C. Lees, *St. Paul's Friends* (London: Religious Tract Society, 1917), 11.

[13] A. W. Tozer, *Let My People Go* (Harrisburg, PA: Christian Publications, 1957), 36.

[14] S. P. Carey, *William Carey* (London: Hodder & Stoughton, 1923), 256.

[15] Lettie B. Cowman, *Charles E. Cowman* (Los Angeles: Oriental Missionary Society, 1928), 269.

[16] Mrs. Hudson Taylor, *Pastor Hsi* (London: China Inland Mission, 1949), 164, 167.

[17] Mark Clark (1896–1984) was a lieutenant general in the U.S. Army during World War II. He commanded the Fifth Army during the Italian campaign and was commander of all United Nations troops in Korea during that conflict.

[18] George Adam Smith, *The Book of Isaiah* (London: Hodder & Stoughton, n.d.), 229.

[19] James Burns, *Revival, Their Laws and Leaders* (London: Hodder & Stoughton, 1909), 311.

[20] *World Vision,* February 1966, 5.

Above All Else

"Choose seven men from among you who are known to be full of the Spirit and wisdom." . . . *They chose Stephen, a man full of faith and of the Holy Spirit.*

—Acts 6:3, 5

Spiritual leadership requires Spirit-filled people. Other qualities are important; to be Spirit-filled is indispensable.

The Book of Acts is the story of people who established the church and led the missionary enterprise. It is of more than passing significance that the central qualification of those who were to occupy even subordinate positions of responsibility in the early church was that they be persons "full of the Holy Spirit." These officers were to be known for integrity and judgment, but preeminently for their spirituality. A person can have a brilliant mind and possess artful administrative skill. But without spirituality he is incapable of giving truly spiritual leadership.

Behind all the busyness of the apostles was the executive activity of the Spirit. As supreme administrator of the church and chief strategist of the missionary enterprise He is everywhere prominent. The Spirit will not delegate authority into secular or carnal hands, even when a particular job has no direct spiritual teaching involved; all workers must be Spirit-led and -filled. Selection of kingdom leaders must not be influenced by worldly wisdom, wealth, or social status. The prime consideration is spirituality. When a church or missions organization follows a different set of criteria, it essentially removes the Spirit from leadership. As a consequence, the Spirit is grieved and quenched, and the result is spiritual dearth and death for that place.

Selecting leaders apart from spiritual qualifications leads always to unspiritual administration. A. T. Pierson compared such a situation to a large corporation that wants to oust its CEO. Slowly, in the board and among the directors and vice-presidents, people are placed who are opposed to the chief's methods and spirit. They quietly antagonize his measures, obstruct his plans, thwart his policy. Where the chief once enjoyed cooperation and support, he now meets inertia and indifference, until at last he resigns from sheer inability to carry out policy.[1] In the same way, appointing leaders with a secular or materialistic outlook prevents the Holy Spirit from making spiritual progress in that place.

The Holy Spirit does not take control of anyone against his or her will. When people who lack spiritual fitness to cooperate with Him are elected to leadership positions, He quietly withdraws and leaves them to implement their own policies according to their own standards, but without His aid. The inevitable result is an unspiritual administration.

The church at Jerusalem listened to the apostles' preaching and selected seven men who possessed the one necessary qualification. As a result of their Spirit-filled work, the church was blessed: the men selected to distribute food and earthly care were soon seen as the Spirit's agents in dispensing heavenly blessings. Stephen became the first martyr for Christ, and his death played a large role in the conversion of Paul. Philip became an evangelist and was used by the Spirit to lead the great revival in Samaria. Leaders who are faithful in the exercise of their gifts prepare the way for promotion to greater responsibilities and usefulness.

The Book of Acts clearly demonstrates that leaders who significantly influenced the Christian movement were Spirit-filled. It is reported of Him who commanded His disciples to tarry in Jerusalem until they were endued with power from on high that He was Himself "anointed . . . with the Holy Spirit and power" (Acts 10:38). Those 120 in the upper room were all filled with the Spirit (2:4). Peter was filled with the Spirit when he addressed the Sanhedrin (4:8). Stephen, filled with the Spirit, bore witness to Christ and died a radiant martyr (6:3-5; 7:55). In the Spirit's fullness Paul began and completed his unique ministry (9:17; 13:9). Paul's missionary companion Barnabas was filled with the Spirit (11:24). We would be strangely blind not to see this obvious requirement for spiritual leadership.

These early leaders of the church were sensitive to the leading of the Spirit. Because they had surrendered their own wills to the Spirit's control, they were delighted to obey His promptings and leadings. Philip left the flourishing revival in Samaria to go to the desert, but what a convert he found there (8:29-39)! The Spirit led Peter to overcome his bias and meet with Cornelius, which led to blessings for the Gentile world (10:9-23; 11:1-18). The Spirit called and sent out Paul and Barnabas as the first missionaries of the church (13:1-4). Throughout his busy life, Paul obeyed the Spirit's restraints and constraints (16:6-8; 19:21; 20:22). The leaders of the church at Jerusalem submitted to the Spirit. "It seemed good to the Holy Spirit and to us" was how the council articulated their judgments (15:28).

The Spirit intervened to bring the gospel to the Gentiles. The Spirit's great purpose is missions. Should that not be ours, too?

Just now as I write, the Spirit is moving among Asian churches, giving them a new missionary vision and passion. For instance, Japanese churches have sent missionaries from Taiwan to Brazil. At a time when the number of North American and European missionaries remains static, the heavenly Strategist is awakening the Asian church to her missionary obligations. Just now more than 3,000 Third World Christians have obeyed the call of God to missions.

Paul counseled leaders in the church at Ephesus on how to understand their office. "Keep watch over yourselves and all the flock of which the Holy Spirit has made you overseers" (Acts 20:28). Those leaders did not hold office by apostolic selection or popular election, but by divine appointment. They were accountable not only to the church, but also to the Holy Spirit. What a sense of assurance and responsibility, what a spiritual authority this teaching brought them—and brings to us!

Without this filling of the Holy Spirit at Pentecost, how could the apostles have faced the superhuman task ahead? They needed superhuman power for their truceless warfare against the devil and hell (Luke 24:49; Eph. 6:10-18).

To be filled with the Spirit means simply that the Christian voluntarily surrenders life and will to the Spirit. Through faith, the believer's personality is filled, mastered, and controlled by the Spirit. The meaning of *filled* is not "to pour into a passive container" but to "take possession of the mind." That's the meaning found in Luke 5:26: "They were filled with awe." When we invite the Spirit to fill us, the Spirit's power grips our lives with this kind of strength and passion.

To be filled with the Spirit is to be controlled by the Spirit. The Christian leader's mind, emotions, will, and physical strength all become available for the Spirit to guide and use. Under the Spirit's control, natural gifts of leadership are lifted to their highest power, sanctified for holy purpose. Through the work of the now ungrieved and unhindered Spirit, all the fruits of the Spirit start to grow in the leader's life. His witness is more winsome, service more steady, and testimony more powerful. All real Christian service is but the expression of the Spirit's power through believers yielded to Him (John 7:37-39).

If we pretend to be filled, or hold back on our willingness to let the Spirit control us, we create the kind of trouble A. W. Tozer warns against:

> No one whose senses have been exercised to know good or evil can but grieve over the sight of zealous souls seeking to be filled with the Holy Spirit while they are living in a state of moral carelessness and borderline sin. Whoever would be indwelt by the Spirit must judge his life for any hidden iniquities. He must expel from his heart everything that is out of accord with the character of God as revealed by the Holy Scriptures. . . . There can be no tolerance of evil, no laughing off the things that God hates.[2]

The filling of the Spirit is essential for spiritual leadership. And each of us is as full of the Spirit as we really want to be.

Complete these sentences:

A. Spiritual leadership requires _____ people.

B. Other qualities are important; to be _____ is indispensable.

Evaluate your church's attitude toward spirituality when selecting leaders.

In your own words, explain what it means to be filled with the Spirit.

Read John 7:37-39.
What is the result of being filled with the Spirit?

How does it affect the work of the church when the leader
has only a secular or materialistic outlook?

Spiritual Gifts

Christians everywhere have undiscovered and unused spiritual gifts. The leader must help bring those gifts into the service of the kingdom, to develop them, to marshal their power. Spirituality alone does not make a leader; natural gifts and those given by God must be there, too.

In our warfare against evil, we need the supernatural equipment God has provided in the spiritual gifts given to the church. To be used effectively, those gifts must be enriched by spiritual grace.

Often, though not always, the Holy Spirit imparts gifts that naturally fit the character and personality of the Christian leader. And the Spirit raises those gifts to a new level of effectiveness. Samuel Chadwick, the noted Methodist preacher, once said that when he was filled with the Spirit, he did not receive a new brain, but a new mentality; not a new tongue, but new speaking effectiveness; not a new language, but a new Bible. Chadwick's natural qualities were given a new vitality, a new energy.

The coming of spiritual gifts in the life of the Christian does not eliminate natural gifts, but enhances and stimulates them. New birth in Christ does not change natural qualities, but when they are placed under the control of the Holy Spirit, they are raised to new effectiveness. Hidden abilities are often released.

The one called by God to spiritual leadership can be confident that the Holy Spirit has given him or her all necessary gifts for the service at hand.

---

[1] A. T. Pierson, *The Acts of the Holy Spirit* (London: Morgan & Scott, n.d.), 63. Arthur Tappan Pierson (1837–1911) was a preacher, writer, and missionary spokesman who also served as a consultant on the Scofield Reference Bible.

[2] D. J. Fant, *A. W. Tozer* (Harrisburg: Christian Publications, 1964), 73, 83.

Prayer and Leadership

I urge, then, first of all, that requests, prayers, intercession and thanksgiving be made for everyone.

—1 Timothy 2:1

The spiritual leader should outpace the rest of the church, above all, in prayer. And yet the most advanced leader is conscious of the possibility of endless development in his prayer life; neither does he ever feel that he has "already attained." Dean C. J. Vaughan once said: "If I wished to humble anyone, I should question him about his prayers. I know nothing to compare with this topic for its sorrowful self-confessions."

Prayer is the most ancient, most universal, and most intensive expression of the religious instinct. It includes the simplest speech of infant lips and the sublime entreaties of older age. All reach the Majesty on high. Prayer is indeed the Christian's vital breath and native air.

But, strange paradox, most of us find it hard to pray. We do not naturally delight in drawing near to God. We sometimes pay lip service to the delight and power of prayer. We call it indispensable; we know the Scriptures call for it. Yet we often fail to pray.

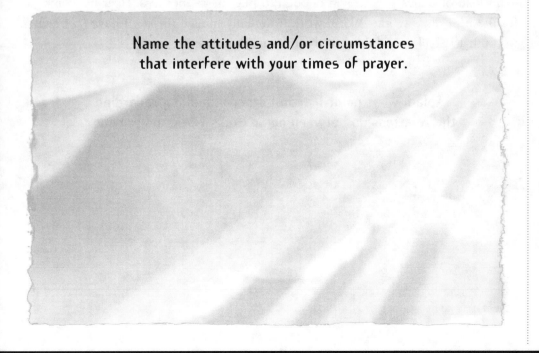

Name the attitudes and/or circumstances that interfere with your times of prayer.

Let us take encouragement from the lives of saintly leaders who overcame this natural reluctance and became mighty in prayer. Of Samuel Chadwick it was said:

> He was essentially a man of prayer. Every morning he would be astir shortly after six o'clock, and he kept a little room which was his private sanctum for his quiet hour before breakfast. He was mighty in public prayer because he was constant in private devotion. . . . When he prayed he expected God to do something. "I wish I had prayed more," he wrote toward the end of his life, "even if I had worked less; and from the bottom of my heart I wish I had prayed better."[1]

"When I go to prayer," confessed an eminent Christian, "I find my heart so loath to go to God, and when it is with Him, so loath to stay." Then self-discipline has a role. "When you feel most indisposed to pray, yield not to it," he counseled, "but strive and endeavor to pray, even when you think you cannot."

What role does self-discipline play in your prayer life?

Mastering the art of prayer, like anything else, takes time. The time we give it will be a true measure of its importance to us. We always find the time for important things. The most common excuse for little time spent in prayer is the list of "to do's" that crowd our day—all our many duties. To Martin Luther, an extra load of duties was reason enough to pray more, not less. Hear his plans for the next day's work: "Work, work from early till late. In fact I have so much to do that I shall spend the first three hours in prayer."

Explain what point Martin Luther is making regarding the relationship between doing God's work and praying.

If Luther was busy, and prayed, so can we.

Try to explain exactly how prayer works and you will quickly run against some difficult puzzles. But people who are skeptical of prayer's validity and power are usually those who do not practice it seriously or fail to obey when God reveals His will. We cannot learn about prayer except by praying. No philosophy has ever taught a soul to pray. The intellectual problems associated with prayer are met in the joy of answered prayer and closer fellowship with God.

The Christian leader who seeks an example to follow does well to turn to the life of Jesus Himself. Our belief in the necessity of prayer comes from observing His life. Surely if anyone could have sustained life without prayer, it would be the very Son of God Himself. If prayer is silly or unnecessary, Jesus would not have wasted His time at it. But wait!

- Prayer was the dominant feature of His life and a recurring part of His teaching.
- Prayer kept His moral vision sharp and clear.
- Prayer gave Him courage to endure the perfect but painful will of His Father.
- Prayer paved the way for transfiguration.

To Jesus, prayer was not a hasty add-on, but a joyous necessity. D.M. McIntyre wrote:

> In Luke 5:16 we have a general statement which throws a vivid light on the daily practice of the Lord. "But He withdrew Himself in the deserts and prayed." It is not of one occasion but of many that the evangelist speaks in this place. It was our Lord's habit to seek retirement for prayer. When He withdrew Himself from men, He was accustomed to press far into the uninhabited country—He was in the deserts. The surprise of the onlookers lay in this, that one so mighty, so richly endowed with spiritual power, should find it necessary for Himself to repair to the source of strength, that there He might refresh His weary spirit. To us, the wonder is still greater, that He, the Prince of Life, the Eternal Word, the Only-begotten of the Father, should prostrate Himself in meekness before the throne of God, making entreaty for grace to help in time of need.[2]

Christ spent full nights in prayer (Luke 6:12). He often rose before dawn to have unbroken communion with His Father (Mark 1:35). The great crises of His life and ministry began with periods of special prayer, as in Luke 5:16: "Jesus often withdrew to lonely places and prayed"—a statement that indicates a regular habit. By word and example He instructed His disciples on the importance of solitude in prayer (Mark 6:46, following the feeding of the five thousand; Luke 9:28, preceding the Transfiguration). To the person on whom devolves the responsibility for selecting personnel for specific spiritual responsibilities, the example of the Lord's spending the night in prayer before making His choice of apostles (Luke 6:12) is luminous.

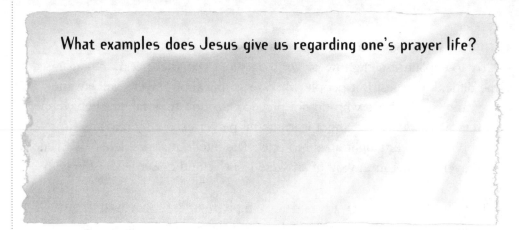

Both our Lord and His bondslave Paul made clear that true prayer is not dreamy reverie. "All vital praying makes a drain on a man's vitality. True intercession is a sacrifice, a bleeding sacrifice," wrote J. H. Jowett. Jesus performed miracles without a sign of outward strain, but "he offered up prayers and petitions with loud cries and tears" (Heb. 5:7).

Sometimes our prayers are pale and weak compared to those of Paul or Epaphras. "Epaphras . . . is always wrestling in prayer for you," wrote Paul in Colossians 4:12. And to the same group: "I want you to know how much I am struggling for you" (Col. 2:1). The Greek word used for "struggle" here is the root for our words *agony* and *agonize*. It is used to describe a person struggling at work until utterly weary (Col. 1:29), or competing in the arena for an athletic prize (1 Cor. 9:25). It describes a soldier battling for his life (1 Tim. 6:12), or a man struggling to deliver his friends from danger (John 18:36). True prayer is a strenuous spiritual exercise that demands the utmost mental discipline and concentration.

We are encouraged to note that Paul, probably the greatest human champion of prayer, confessed, "We do not know what we ought to pray for." And then he hastened to add, "The Spirit himself intercedes for us with groans that words cannot express. And he who searches our hearts knows the mind of the Spirit, because the Spirit intercedes for the saints in accordance with God's will" (Rom. 8:26-27). The Spirit joins us in prayer and pours His supplications into our own.

All Christians need more teaching in the art of prayer, and the Holy Spirit is the master teacher. The Spirit's help in prayer is mentioned in the Bible more frequently than any other help He gives us. All true praying comes from the Spirit's activity in our souls. Both Paul and Jude teach that effective prayer is "praying in the Spirit." That phrase means that we pray along the same lines, about the same things, in the same name, as the Holy Spirit. True prayer rises in the spirit of the Christian from the Spirit who indwells us.

To pray in the Spirit is important for two reasons. First, we are to pray in the realm of the Spirit, for the Holy Spirit is the sphere and atmosphere of the Christian's life. In this we often fail. Much praying is psychical rather than spiritual, in the realm of the mind alone, the product of our own thinking and not of the Spirit's teaching. But real prayer is deeper. It uses the body, requires the cooperation of the mind, and moves in the supernatural realm of the Spirit. Such praying transacts its business in the heavenly realm.

Explain how we are to pray in the Spirit.

1. In the _____ or the Spirit:

2. In the _____ and _____ of the Spirit:

Second, we are to pray in the power and energy of the Spirit. "Give yourselves wholly to prayer and entreaty; pray on every occasion in the power of the Spirit" (Eph. 6:18, NEB). For its superhuman task, prayer demands more than human power. We have the Spirit of power as well as the Spirit of prayer. All the human energy of heart, mind, and will can achieve great human results; but praying in the Holy Spirit releases supernatural resources.

The Spirit delights to help us pray. In each of our three chief handicaps, we can count on the Spirit's help. Sometimes we are kept from prayer by sin in our heart. As we grow in trust and submission, the Holy Spirit leads us to the blood of Christ, which cleanses every stain.

Sometimes the ignorance of our minds hinders our prayers. But the Spirit knows the mind of God and shares that knowledge with us as we wait and listen. The Spirit does this by giving us a clear conviction that a particular prayer request is part of God's will for us, or not.

Sometimes we are earthbound because of the infirmity of the body. We get sick, we feel ill, we are weak. The Spirit will quicken our bodies and enable us to rise above weaknesses, even those imposed by sultry tropical climates.

Then, as if these three conditions were not enough, the spiritual leader must oppose Satan in prayer. Satan will try to depress, to create doubt and discouragement, to keep a leader from communion with God. In the Holy Spirit, we have a heavenly ally against this supernatural foe.

Spiritual leaders should know the experience of praying in the Spirit as part of their daily walk. Do we ever try to live independently of the Spirit? Do we fail to see full answers to prayer? We can read all day about prayer and experience little of its power, and so stunt our service.

The Bible often explains prayer as spiritual warfare. "For our struggle is . . . against the rulers, against the authorities, against the powers of this dark world and against the spiritual forces of evil in the heavenly realms" (Eph. 6:12). In this struggle phase of prayer, three personalities are engaged. Between God and the devil stands the Christian at prayer. Though weak alone, the Christian plays a strategic role in the struggle between the dragon and the Lamb. The praying Christian wields no personal power and authority, but authority delegated by the victorious Christ to whom that faithful believer is united by faith. Faith is like a network through which the victory won on Calvary reaches the devil's captives and delivers them from darkness into light.

Jesus was not so much concerned over wicked people and their deeds as with the forces of evil that caused those people to sin. Behind Peter's denial and Judas's betrayal was the sinister hand of Satan. "Get thee behind me, Satan," was the Lord's response to Peter's presumptuous rebuke. All around us are people bound in sin, captives to the devil. Our prayers should ascend not only for them, but against Satan, who holds them as his prize. Satan must be compelled to relax his grip, and this can only be achieved by Christ's victory on the cross.

How does prayer fit into the battle against Satan?

Make a list of those for whom you are praying for a release from Satan's grip.

As Jesus dealt with sin's cause rather than effect, so the spiritual leader should adopt the same method in prayer. And the leader must know how to help those following along in that same spiritual warfare.

In a telling illustration, Jesus compared Satan to a strong man, fully armed. Before anyone can enter such a man's house and set captives free, the man must first be bound. Only then can a rescue succeed (Matt. 12:29). What could it mean to "tie up the strong man" except to neutralize his might through the overcoming power of Christ who came "to destroy (nullify, render inoperative) the works of the devil"? And how can that happen except by the prayer of faith that lays hold of the victory of Calvary and claims it for the problem at hand? We cannot hope to effect a rescue from Satan's den without first disarming the adversary. God opens His divine authority through prayer, and we can confidently claim it. Jesus promised His disciples: "I have given you authority . . . to overcome all the power of the enemy" (Luke 10:19).

The spiritual leader will be alert to the most effective way to influence people. Hudson Taylor is well known for his expression, "It is possible to move men, through God, by prayer alone." During his missionary career he demonstrated the truth of his claim a thousand times.

It is one thing to believe such power is available, but another thing to practice it. People are difficult to move; it is much easier to pray for things or provisions than to deal with the stubbornness of the human heart. But in just these intricate situations the leader must use God's power to move human hearts in the direction he believes to be the will of God. Through prayer the leader has the key to that complicated lock.

It is the supreme dignity and glory of the human creature to be able to say yes or no to God. Humans have been given free will. But this poses a problem. If by prayer we can influence the conduct of others, does such power encroach on free will? Will God temper one person's freedom to answer another person's prayer? It seems difficult to imagine. And yet, if prayers cannot influence the course of events, why pray?

The first point to make is that God is consistent with Himself always. God does not contradict Himself. When God promises to answer prayer, the answer will come always in a manner consistent with divine nature, for "he cannot disown himself" (2 Tim. 2:13). No word or action from God will contradict any other word or action.

The second point in resolving these questions is that intercessory prayer is a divine ordinance. God has ordained prayer, and we can be confident that as we meet revealed conditions for prayer, answers will be granted. God sees no contradiction between human free will and divine response to prayer. When God commands us to pray "for kings and those in authority," there is implied power to influence the course of men and events. If not, why pray? Our obligation to pray stands above any dilemma concerning the effects of prayer.

Third, we can know the will of God concerning the prayer we raise. Our capacity to know God's will is the basis for all prayers of faith. God can speak to us clearly through our minds and hearts. The Bible instructs us directly concerning the will of God on all matters of principle. In our hearts the Holy Spirit ministers to instruct us in the will of God (Rom. 8:26-27). As we patiently seek the will of God concerning our petition, the Spirit will impress our minds and convince our hearts. Such God-given conviction leads us beyond the prayer of hope to the prayer of faith.

Recap the three points which answer the question: Why can prayer move human hearts in the direction of the will of God?

1.

2.

3.

When God lays a burden on our hearts and thus keeps us praying, He obviously intends to grant the answer. George Mueller was asked if he really believed that two men would be converted, men for whom Mueller had prayed over 50 years. Mueller replied: "Do you think God would have kept me praying all these years if He did not intend to save them?" In fact, both men were converted, one shortly after Mueller's death.[3]

In prayer we deal directly with God and only in a secondary sense other people. The goal of prayer is the ear of God. Prayer moves others through God's influence on them. It is not the prayer that moves people, but the God to whom we pray.

> Prayer moves the arm
> That moves the world
> To bring deliverance down.
> —Author unknown

To move people, the leader must be able to move God, for God has made it clear that He moves people in response to prayer. If a scheming Jacob was given "power with God and with men" (Gen. 32:28, KJV), then surely any leader who follows God's prayer principles can enjoy the same power.

Prevailing prayer that moves people is the outcome of a correct relationship with God. The Bible is very clear on the reasons why prayers go unanswered, and every reason centers on the believer's relationship with God. God will not cooperate with prayers of mere self-interest, or prayers that come from impure motives. The Christian who clings to sin closes the ear of God. Least of all will God tolerate unbelief, the chief of sins. "Anyone who comes to him must believe" (Heb. 11:6). In all our prayers the paramount motive is the glory of God.

Great leaders of the Bible were great at prayer. "They were not leaders because of brilliancy of thought, because they were exhaustless in resources, because of their magnificent culture or native endowment, but because, by the power of prayer, they could command the power of God."[4]

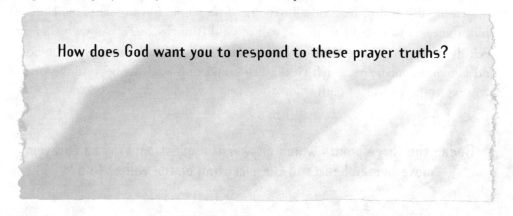

How does God want you to respond to these prayer truths?

[1] N. G. Dunning, *Samuel Chadwick* (London: Hodder & Stoughton, 1934), 19.

[2] D. M. McIntyre, *The Prayer Life of Our Lord* (London: Morgan & Scott, n.d.), 30–31.

[3] George Mueller (1805–1898) was a Plymouth Brethren leader who refused a salary, believing that God would supply his needs by prayer alone. He established an orphanage in Bristol for 2,000 youngsters on the strength of prayer and promoted prayer during a 17-year world tour.

[4] E. M. Bounds, *Prayer and Praying Men* (London: Hodder & Stoughton, 1921). Edward McKendree Bounds (1835–1913) was an American Methodist Episcopal minister who served churches throughout the South. He was a captain in the Confederate army.

The Leader and Time

Make the best use of your time.
>—Ephesians 5:16, Phillips

The quality of a person's leadership depends on what happens during time. The character and career of a young person depends on how he or she spends spare time. We cannot regulate school or office hours—those are determined for us—but we can say what we will do before and after. The way we employ the surplus hours after provision has been made for work, meals, and sleep will determine if we develop into mediocre or powerful people. Leisure is a glorious opportunity and a subtle danger. Each moment of the day is a gift from God that deserves care; for by any measure, our time is short and the work is great.

What guides do you follow to "make the best use of your time"?

Minutes and hours wisely used translate into an abundant life. On one occasion when Michelangelo was pressing himself to finish a work on deadline, someone warned him, "This may cost your life!" He replied, "What else is life for?"

Hours and days will surely pass, but we can direct them purposefully and productively. Philosopher William James affirmed that the best use of one's life is to spend it for something that will outlast it. Life's value is not its duration but its donation—not how long we live, but how fully and how well.[1]

Time is precious, but we squander it thoughtlessly. Moses knew time was valuable and prayed to be taught to measure it by days, not by years (Ps. 90:12). If we are careful about days, the years will take care of themselves.

A leader will seldom say, "I don't have the time." Such an excuse is usually the refuge of a small-minded and inefficient person. Each of us has the time to do the whole will of God for our lives. J. H. Jowett said:

I think one of the can't phrases of our day is the familiar one by which we express our permanent want of time. We repeat it so often that by the very repetition we have deceived ourselves into believing it. *It is never the supremely busy men who have no time.* So compact and systematic is the regulation of their day that whenever you make a demand on them, they seem to find additional corners to offer for unselfish service. I confess as a minister, that the men to whom I most hopefully look for additional service are the busiest men.

Our problem is not too little time, but making better use of the time we have. Each of us has as much time as anyone else. The president of the United States has the same 24 hours as we. Others may surpass our abilities, influence, or money; but no one has more time.

What circumstances and/or attitudes rob you of time well spent?

As in the parable of the pounds ("minas" in the NIV; Luke 19:12-27), where each servant was given the same amount of money, we each have been given the same amount of time. But few of us use it so wisely as to produce a tenfold return. The parable recognizes different abilities; the servant with less capacity but equal faithfulness received the same reward. We are not responsible for our endowments or natural abilities, but we are responsible for the strategic use of time.

When Paul urged the Ephesians to "redeem" the time (see 5:16, KJV), he was treating time like a purchase. We exchange time in the market of life for certain occupations and activities that may be worthy or not, productive or not. Another translation renders the verse, "Buy up the opportunities," for time is opportunity. Herein lies the importance of a carefully planned life: "If we progress in the economy of time, we are learning to live. If we fail here, we fail everywhere."

Time lost can never be retrieved. Time cannot be hoarded, only spent well. These lines were found engraved on a sundial:

> The shadow of my finger cast
> Divides the future from the past;
>   Before it stands the unborn hour
>   In darkness and beyond thy power;
> Behind its unreturning line
> The vanished hour, no longer thine;
>   One hour alone is in thy hands,
>   The now on which the shadow stands.
> —Author Unknown

In the face of this sobering reality, the leader must carefully select priorities. He or she must thoughtfully weigh the value of different opportunities and responsibilities. The leader cannot spend time on secondary matters while essential obligations scream for attention. A day needs careful planning. The person who wants to excel must select and reject, then concentrate on the most important items.

Identify the steps you take to prioritize your responsibilities.

It is often helpful to keep records of how each hour in a given week is spent, and then look at the record in the light of scriptural priorities. The results may be shocking. Often the record shows that we have much more time available for Christian service than we imagine.

On a separate sheet of paper, record the past two days of your life hour by hour.

1. How much time did you spend alone with God?

2. How much time did you spend in Christian service?

3. What or who took up time you had already scheduled?

4. In what other ways could you have handled the events in question 3?

Suppose that we allot ourselves a generous eight hours a day for sleep (and few need more than that), three hours for meals and conversation, ten hours for work and travel on five days. Still we have 35 hours each week to fill. What happens to them? How are they invested? A person's entire contribution to the kingdom of God may turn on how those hours are used. Certainly those hours determine whether life is commonplace or extraordinary.

The intrepid missionary Mary Slessor was the daughter of a drunkard. At age 11 she began working in a factory in Dundee, and there spent her days from six in the morning until six at night. Yet that grueling regimen did not prevent her from educating herself for a notable career.[2]

David Livingstone, at age 10, worked in a cotton mill in Dumbarton 14 hours a day. Surely he had excuses for not studying, for not redeeming the little leisure left to him. But he learned Latin and could read Horace and Virgil at age 16. At age 27, he had finished a program in both medicine and theology.

Similar examples are so numerous that we have little ground today to plead insufficient time for achieving something worthwhile in life.

Our Lord sets the perfect example of strategic use of time. He moved through life with measured steps, never hurried, though always surrounded by demands and crowds. When a person approached Him for help, Jesus gave the impression that He had no more important concern than the needs of His visitor.

The secret of Jesus' serenity lay in His assurance that He was working according to the Father's plan for His life—a plan that embraced every hour and made provision for every contingency. Through communion in prayer with His Father, Jesus received each day both the words He would say and the works He would do. "The words I say to you are not just my own. Rather, it is the Father, living in me, who is doing his work" (John 14:10).

What can you learn from Jesus' example of time management?

Jesus' greatest concern was to fulfill the work committed to Him within the allotted hours. He was conscious of a divine timing in His life (John 7:6; 12:23, 27; 13:1; 17:1). Even to His beloved mother He said, "My time has not yet come" (2:4). Responding to Mary and Martha's distress, Jesus declined to change His schedule by two days (11:1-6). When He reviewed His life at its close, He said: "I have brought you glory on earth by completing the work you gave me to do" (17:4). Jesus completed His life's work without any part spoiled by undue haste or half-done through lack of time. His 24 hours a day were sufficient to complete the whole will of God.

Jesus told His disciples: "Are there not twelve hours in the day?" J. Stuart Holden saw in our Lord's words both the shortness of time and the sufficiency of time. There were indeed 12 hours in the day, but in fact there were fully 12 hours in the day.[3]

Conscious of time, Jesus spent His time doing things that mattered. No time was wasted on things not vital. The strength of moral character is conserved by refusing the unimportant.

> No trifling in this life of mine;
> Not this the path the blessed Master trod;
> But every hour and power employed
> Always and all for God.
> —Author unknown

How interesting that the Gospel accounts contain no hint of any interruption ever disturbing the serenity of the Son of God. Few things are more likely to produce tension in a busy life than unexpected interruptions. Yet to Jesus there were no such things. "Unexpected" events were always foreseen in the Father's planning, and Jesus was therefore undisturbed by them. True, at times there was hardly time to eat; but time was always sufficient to accomplish all the Father's will.

Often the pressure a spiritual leader feels comes from assuming tasks that God has not assigned; for such tasks the leader cannot expect God to supply the extra strength required.

Name any tasks that you currently are assuming that are not part of God's assignment for you.

One busy man told me how he mastered the problem of interruptions. "Up to some years ago," he testified, "I was always annoyed by them, which was really a form of selfishness on my part. People used to walk in and say, 'Well, I just had two hours to kill here in between trains, and I thought I would come and see you.' That used to bother me. Then the Lord convinced me that He sends people our way. He sent Philip to the Ethiopian eunuch. He sent Barnabas to see Saul. The same applies today. God sends people our way.

"So when someone comes in, I say, 'The Lord must have brought you here. Let us find out why He sent you. Let us have prayer.' Well, this does two things. The interview takes on new importance because God is in it. And it generally shortens the interview. If a visitor knows you are looking for reasons why God should have brought him, and there are none apparent, the visit becomes pleasant but brief.

"So now I take interruptions as from the Lord. They belong in my schedule, because the schedule is God's to arrange at His pleasure."

Paul affirms that God has a plan for every life. We have been "created in Christ Jesus to do good works, which God prepared in advance for us to do" (Eph. 2:10). Through daily prayer, the leader discovers the details of that plan and arranges work accordingly. Each half hour should carry its load of usefulness.

What changes can you make to master the problem of interruption?

John Wesley and F. B. Meyer, men who influenced the world for Christ, divided their days into five-minute periods, then tried to make each one count.[4] All of us could benefit by similar discipline. For example, much reading can be done during otherwise wasted minutes.

Meyer's biographer tells how he would redeem the time:

> If he had a long railway journey before him, he would settle himself in his corner of the railway carriage, open his dispatch case which was fitted as a sort of stationery cabinet, and set to work on some abstruse article, quite oblivious of his surroundings. Often at protracted con-

ventions, and even in committee meetings, when the proceeding did not demand his undivided attention, he would unobtrusively open his case and proceed to answer letters.

Another miser with time was W. E. Sangster. His son wrote of him:

Time was never wasted. The difference between one minute and two was of considerable consequence to him. He would appear from his study. "My boy, you're not doing anything. I have exactly twenty-two minutes. We'll go for a walk. We can walk right around the common in that time." He then hurtled out of the house at tremendous speed and I normally had to run to catch up. He would then discourse on current affairs (five minutes), Surrey's prospects in the country championship (two minutes), the necessity for revival (five minutes), the reality of the Loch Ness monster (two minutes), and the sanctity of William Romaine (three minutes). By that time we would be home again.[5]

A leader needs a balanced approach to time lest it become his bondage and downfall. Without a grip on time, the leader works under unnecessary strain. Even when the leader has done the utmost to fulfill daily obligations, vast areas of work always remain. Every call for help is not necessarily a call from God, for it is impossible to respond to every need. If the leader sincerely plans his day in prayer, then executes the plan with all energy and eagerness, that is enough. A leader is responsible only for what lies within the range of control. The rest he should trust to our loving and competent heavenly Father.

Procrastination, the thief of time, is one of the devil's most potent weapons for defrauding us of eternal heritage. The habit of "putting off" is fatal to spiritual leadership. Its power resides in our natural reluctance to come to grips with important decisions. Making decisions and acting on them always requires moral energy. But the passing of time never makes action easier—quite the opposite. Most decisions are more difficult a day later, and you may also lose an advantage by such delay. The nettle will never be easier to grasp than now.

"Do it now" is a motto that has led many people to worldly success, and it is equally relevant in spiritual matters. A helpful method for overcoming procrastination is to set deadlines and never miss or postpone even one.

How does the sovereignty of God figure into your daily schedule?

---

[1] Michelangelo (1475–1564) was an Italian sculptor, painter, and poet. His famous works include the statue of David and the ceiling of the Sistine Chapel in the Vatican. William James (1842–1910) was a Harvard psychologist and philosopher generally credited with popularizing a new approach to knowledge called pragmatism.

[2] Mary Slessor (1848–1915) went to Calabar, West Africa, in 1876, a region not controlled by any colonial power. She contributed immensely to the life of children and women there.

[3] J. Stuart Holden, *The Gospel of the Second Chance* (London: Marshall Brothers, 1912), 188.

[4] W. Y. Fullerton, *F. B. Meyer* (London: Marshall, Morgan & Scott, n.d.), 70. Frederick Brotherton Meyer (1847–1929) was a Baptist preacher with a worldwide pulpit and a base in London. John Wesley (1703–91) is well known as the energetic cofounder of Methodism.

[5] Paul E. Sangster, *Doctor Sangster* (London: Epworth, 1962), 314.

The Leader and Reading

When you come, bring. . . my scrolls, especially the parchments.
—2 Timothy 4:13

Reading maketh a full man; speaking, a ready man, writing, an exact man.
—Francis Bacon

Paul's counsel to Timothy, "Give heed to reading," surely referred to the public reading of the Old Testament. But Paul's advice is most appropriate for other areas of reading as well. Paul's books—the ones he wanted Timothy to bring along—were probably works of Jewish history, explanations of the law and prophets, and perhaps some of the heathen poets Paul quoted in his sermons and lectures. A student to the end, Paul wanted to spend time in study.

During his imprisonment and shortly before his martyrdom in 1536, William Tyndale wrote to the governor-in-chief asking that some goods be sent him:

> A warmer cap, a candle, a piece of cloth to patch my leggings. . . .
> But above all, I beseech and entreat your clemency to be urgent
> with the Procureur that he may kindly permit me to have my
> Hebrew Bible, Hebrew grammar and Hebrew Dictionary, that I may
> spend time with that in study.[1]

Both Paul and Tyndale devoted their last days on earth to the study of the parchments. Spiritual leaders of every generation will have a consuming passion to know the Word of God through diligent study and the illumination of the Holy Spirit. But in this chapter our special interest is a leader's supplementary reading

The leader who intends to grow spiritually and intellectually will be reading constantly. Lawyers must read steadily to keep up on case law. Doctors must read to stay current in the ever-changing world of health care. So the spiritual leader must master God's Word and its principles and know as well the minds of those who look to the leader for guidance. To do so, the leader must have an active life of reading.

Prepare a list of 10 books you have read in the last year.

1.

2.

3.

4.

5.

6.

7.

8.

9.

10.

Today the practice of reading spiritual classics is on the wane. We have more leisure today than ever before in history, but many people claim to have no time for reading. A spiritual leader cannot use that excuse.

John Wesley had a passion for reading, and he did so mostly on horseback. Often he rode a horse 50 and sometimes 90 miles in a day. His habit was to ride with a volume of science or history or medicine propped in the pommel of his saddle, and thus he consumed thousands of books. Besides his Greek New Testament, three great books took possession of Wesley's mind and heart during his Oxford days: *Imitation of Christ, Holy Living and Dying,* and *The Serious Call.* These three were his spiritual guides. Wesley told the younger ministers of the Methodist societies to read or get out of the ministry!

Circle the title(s) of any of the three books that influenced Wesley which you have read.

Leaders should determine to spend a minimum of half an hour a day reading books that feed the soul and stimulate the mind. In a perceptive series on "The Use and Abuse of Books," A. W. Tozer said:

> Why does today's Christian find the reading of great books always beyond him? Certainly intellectual powers do not wane from one generation to another. We are as smart as our fathers, and any thought they could entertain we can entertain if we are sufficiently interested to make the effort. The major cause of the decline in the quality of current Christian literature is not intellectual but spiritual. To enjoy a great religious book requires a degree of consecration to God and detachment from the world that few modern Christians have. The early Christian Fathers, the Mystics, the Puritans, are not hard to understand, but they inhabit the highlands where the air is crisp and rarefied, and

none but the God-enamored can come. . . . One reason why people are unable to understand great Christian classics is that they are trying to understand without any intention of obeying them.[2]

Why Read?

"Read to refill the wells of inspiration," was the advice of Harold Ockenga, who took a suitcase of books on his honeymoon![3]

Bacon's famous rule for reading: "Read not to contradict or confute, nor to believe and take for granted, nor to find talk and discourse, but to weigh and consider. Some books are to be tested, others to be swallowed, and some few to be chewed and digested."[4] Indeed, if we read merely to stock our head with ideas, to feel superior to others, or to appear learned, then our reading is useless and vain.

The spiritual leader should choose books for their spiritual benefit. Some authors challenge heart and conscience and point us toward the highest; they spark our impulse to service and lead us to God.

Spiritual leaders should also read for intellectual growth. This will require books that test wits, provide fresh ideas, challenge assumptions, and probe complexities.

The leader should read to cultivate his preaching and writing style. For that, nothing can equal the writing of those masters who enlarge our vocabularies, teach us to think, and instruct us in the art of incisive and compelling speech. Tozer recommended John Bunyan for simplicity, Joseph Addison for clarity and elegance, John Milton for nobility and consistent elevation of thought, Charles Dickens for sprightliness, and Francis Bacon for dignity.

The leader should read, too, to acquire new information, to keep current with the time, to be well-informed in his or her own field of expertise.

The leader should read to have fellowship with great minds. Through books we hold communion with the greatest spiritual leaders of the ages.

A good book has great power. In *Curiosities of Literature*, Benjamin Disraeli gives a number of instances where a person has been magnificently influenced by a solitary book. As I have read the biographies of great Christians, time and again one book has brought their lives to crisis and produced a revolution of ministry. That book is Charles G. Finney's *Lectures on Revivals of Religion*.[5]

Explain why spiritual leaders should read supplementary books.

What to Read

If a man is known by the company he keeps, so also his character is reflected in the books he reads. A leader's reading is the outward expression of his inner hungers and aspirations. The vast number of titles pouring from presses today makes discriminating choice essential. We can afford to read only the best, only that which invigorates our mission. Our reading should be regulated by who we are and what we intend to accomplish.

An old author whose pen name was Cladius Clear said that a reader could divide his books as he would people. A few were "lovers," and those books would go with him into exile. Others were "friends." Most books were "acquaintances," works with which he was on nodding terms.

Matthew Arnold thought that the best of literature was bound within five hundred book covers. Daniel Webster preferred to master a few books rather than read widely. To them he would appeal for genuine knowledge of the human heart, its aspirations and tragedies, hopes and disappointments. Indiscriminate reading serves no one well. Hobbes, the English philosopher, once said, "If I had read as many books as other people, I would know as little."

Samuel Brengle said this about poetry:

> I like the poets whose writings reveal great moral character and passion such as Tennyson's and some of Browning's. The works of others have light, but I prefer flame to just light. Shakespeare? A mind as clear as a sunbeam—but passionless, light without heat. Shelley? Keats? There's a sense in which they were perfect poets, but they don't move me. Beautiful—but wordmongers. There's an infinite difference between the beauty of holiness and the holiness of beauty. One leads to the highest, loftiest, most Godlike character; the other often—too often—leads to an orgy of sensation.[6]

Sir W. Robertson Nicoll, for many years editor of *British Weekly*, found biography the most attractive form of general reading because biography transmits personality. To read the lives of great and consecrated men and women is to kindle one's own heart toward God. Imagine how the missions movement has been inspired by the biographies of William Carey, Adoniram Judson, Hudson Taylor, Charles Studd, and Albert Simpson.[7]

Joseph W. Kemp, widely known for his preaching and teaching, always kept a good biography on hand. Ransome W. Cooper wrote:

> The reading of good biography forms an important part of a Christian's education. It provides him with numberless illustrations for use in his own service. He learns to assess the true worth of character, to glimpse a work goal for his own life, to decide how best to attain it, what self-denial is needed to curb unworthy aspirations; and all the time he learns how God breaks into the dedicated life to bring about his own purposes.

A leader should neither be content with easy books nor satisfied with reading only in his specialty. Muriel Ormrod counseled:

> It is better that we should always tackle something a bit beyond us. We should always aim to read something different—not only

the writers with whom we agree, but those with whom we are ready to do battle. And let us not condemn them out of hand because they do not agree with us; their point of view challenges us to examine the truth and to test their views against Scripture. And let us not comment on nor criticize writers of whom we have heard only second-hand, or third-hand, without troubling to read their works for ourselves. . . . Don't be afraid of new ideas—and don't be carried away with them either.[8]

The leader should immerse himself in books that equip him for higher service and leadership in the kingdom of God.

> A little learning is a dangerous thing;
> Drink deep, or taste not the Pierian Spring;
> There shallow draughts intoxicate the brain,
> And drinking largely sobers us again.
> —Alexander Pope

How to Read

By reading we learn. By meditating on the themes of our reading we pluck the fruit from the tree of books and add nourishment to our minds and our ministries. Unless our reading includes serious thinking, it is wasted time.

When Southey, the poet, was telling a Quaker lady how he learned Portuguese grammar while he washed, and French literature while he dressed, and science while he took breakfast, and so on, filling his day utterly, she said quietly, "And when does thee think?" We can read without thinking, but such reading has no profit for us. Spurgeon counseled his students:

> Master those books you have. Read them thoroughly. Bathe in them until they saturate you. Read and reread them, masticate and digest them. Let them go into your very self. Peruse a good book several times and make notes and analyses of it. A student will find that his mental constitution is more affected by one book thoroughly mastered than by twenty books he has merely skimmed. Little learning and much pride comes of hasty reading. Some men are disabled from thinking by their putting meditation away for the sake of much reading. In reading let your motto be "much, not many."[9]

Use these rules for making your reading worthwhile and profitable:

- What you intend to quickly forget, spend little time reading. The habit of reading and forgetting only builds the habit of forgetting other important matters.
- Use the same discrimination in choosing books as in choosing friends.
- Read with pencil and notebook in hand. Unless your memory is unusually retentive, much gained from reading is lost in a day. Develop a system of note-taking. It will greatly help the memory.
- Have a "commonplace book," as they are called—a book to record what is striking, interesting, and worthy of second thought. In that way you will build a treasure trove of material for future use.

- Verify historical, scientific, and other data.
- Pass no word until its meaning is known.
- Vary your reading to keep your mind out of a rut. Variety is as refreshing to the mind as it is to the body.
- Correlate your reading—history with poetry, biography with historical novel. For example, when reading the history of the American Civil War, take up the biography of Lincoln or Grant and the poetry of Whitman.

Canon Yates advised that every good book needs three readings. The first should be rapid and continuous, to give your mind an overview and to associate the book's material with your previous knowledge. The second reading should be careful and paced. Take notes and think. Then after an interval of time, a third reading should be like the first. Write a brief analysis of the book on the inside back cover. Thus will the book make a solid imprint on your memory.

A Scottish minister in Lumsden town had collected 17,000 volumes, which he browsed with great delight. But his son said later, "Though he spent much time and pains on his sermons, he did not cut a channel between them and his reading."[10]

Beware the danger of the Lumsden syndrome. A book is a channel for the flow of ideas between one mind and another. The Lumsden preacher may have had the benefit of books for his own spiritual life, but the people in his church apparently never felt the influence of his reading. Leaders should always cut a channel between reading and speaking and writing, so that others derive benefit, pleasure, and inspiration.

A country minister in Australia known to this writer was a great book lover. Early in his ministry he determined to develop a biblically and theologically literate congregation. He helped his people learn to love books and led them into progressively deeper and weightier spiritual literature. The result is that a number of farmers in that district have significant libraries and thoughtful faith.

More ministers should try to lead in this way, guiding the church toward intelligent reading and larger, more committed, more resilient faith.

---

[1] William Tyndale (c. 1494–1536) was the first to translate the New Testament into English, in 1525, from a base in Germany. He was arrested in 1535 and a year later burned at the stake. Before his death, he completed the translation of the first five Old Testament books and Jonah.

[2] A. W. Tozer, "The Use and Abuse of Books," *The Alliance Weekly*, 22 February 1956, 2.

[3] Harold J. Ockenga, *Christianity Today,* 4 March 1966, 36.

[4] Francis Bacon, quoted in *The Alliance Weekly*, 14 March 1956, 2. Bacon (1561–1626) was a statesman and scholar who served Elizabeth I and James I. His many writings deal with scientific method, political theory, and the history of ideas. He was a loyal member of the Church of England.

[5] Charles Finney (1792–1875) was trained in law but turned to ministry after his conversion in 1821. He led revivals through the Northeast, pastored churches, wrote books, opposed slavery and drink, and was president of Oberlin College from 1851–66. The book cited here was published in 1835.

[6] C. W. Hall, *Samuel Logan Brengle* (New York: Salvation Army, 1933), 269.

[7] Charles Thomas Studd (1862–1931) inherited a fortune, but gave it away and sailed to China as a missionary in 1885. He also served in India and Africa, and helped found the Student Volunteer Movement.

[8] Muriel Ormrod, *The Reaper*, August 1965, 229.

[9] Helmut Thielecke, *Encounter with Spurgeon* (Philadelphia: Fortress, 1963), 197.

[10] *The Sunday School Times,* 22 November 1913, 715.

Improving Leadership

If you are a leader, exert yourself to lead.
—Romans 12:8, NEB

Every Christian is obliged to be the best he can be for God. Like any other worthwhile activity, if leadership can be improved, we should seek to improve it. In so doing, we prepare ourselves for higher service that may be just around the next corner, though unseen at the present.

Not every Christian is called to major leadership in the church, but every Christian is a leader, for we all influence others. All of us should strive to improve our leadership potential.

The first step toward improvement is to recognize weaknesses, make corrections, and cultivate strengths. Many reasons explain why church leadership is less than the best, and perhaps some of these apply to you.

- Perhaps we lack a clearly defined goal that will stretch us, challenge faith, and unify life's activities.
- Perhaps our faith is timid, and we hesitate to take risks for the kingdom.
- Do we show the zeal of salvation in Christ, or is our demeanor morbid and sad? Enthusiastic leaders generate enthusiastic followers.
- We may be reluctant to grasp the nettle of a difficult situation and deal courageously with it. Or we may procrastinate, hoping that problems will vanish with time. The mediocre leader postpones difficult decisions, conversation, and letters. Delay solves nothing and usually makes problems worse.
- Perhaps we sacrifice depth for breadth, and spreading ourselves thin, achieve only superficial results.

Exert Yourself to Lead

Romans 12:1 issues this imperative to leaders: "Offer your bodies as living sacrifices, holy and pleasing to God." The Greek aorist tense of the verb "offer" (which signifies a one-time act that is finished and done) is followed by 36 present-tense verbs (continuous action) that specify what happens when we obey and offer. Two of those results are especially noteworthy here.

First, "exert yourself to lead" (Rom. 12:8, NEB). Barclay translates this phrase, "If called upon to supply leadership, do it with zeal." Here is the summons to dive wholeheartedly into leadership, to serve with energy, to leave no room for sloth. Are we doing it?

Does your leadership show the intensity typical of Jesus? When the disciples saw the Master ablaze with righteous anger at the desecration of His Father's temple, they remembered the writings: "Zeal for your house will consume me" (John 2:17; cf. Ps. 69:9). So strong was Jesus' zeal that His friends thought He had abandoned common sense (Mark 3:21) and His enemies charged Him with having a demon (John 7:20).

Similar intensity marked Paul at every stage of his life. Adolph Deissman wrote:

> The lightning of the Damascus road found plenty of flammable material in the soul of the young persecutor. We see the flames shoot up, and we feel the glow then kindled lost none of its brightness in Paul the aged.

We should strive for such continuing intensity as we grow older. Age tends to turn a flame into embers—the fire needs fresh fuel always.

Before his conversion, Paul's zeal drove him to terrible cruelty against the early Christians, such that he mourned of it later. That same zeal, cleansed by the Holy Spirit, carried into his new life in Christ and led to amazing achievements for the very church he once tried to destroy.

Because he was constantly full of the Spirit, Paul's mind was aflame with the truth of God and his heart glowed with God's love. At the center of his life was passion for the glory of God. No wonder people followed Paul. He exerted himself to lead. He did it with intensity and zeal. And the spirit of his life was contagious to those around him.

Kept at Boiling Point

Our second present-tense verb in Romans 12 comes from verse 11: "Never be lacking in zeal, but keep your spiritual fervor, serving the Lord." Harrington Lees translates this verse: "Not slothful in business, kept at boiling point by the Holy Spirit, doing bondservice for the master."

This verse points to the dynamic for consistent, zealous service: "Kept at boiling point by the Holy Spirit." For most people in leadership, boiling points come easily on special occasions. Most leaders know times of great spiritual excitement, of the burning heart, of special nearness to God and more than ordinary fruitfulness in service—but the problem is staying there! Verse 11 holds out the alluring possibility of living "aglow with the Spirit" (RSV). We need not go off boil if the Spirit is the great central furnace of our lives.

Bunyan's Christian discovered this secret while visiting the Interpreter's house. He could not understand how the flames kept leaping higher while someone poured water on them. Then he saw another toward the rear pouring on the oil.[1]

In His great sermon on prayer in Luke 11, Jesus promised that the Holy Spirit would be given if only we ask. He said, "If you then, though you are evil, know how to give good gifts to your children, how much more will your Father in heaven give the Holy Spirit to those who ask him!" (Luke 11:13). When we trust Christ for salvation, this promise is fulfilled in us, for Paul teaches that "if anyone does not have the Spirit of Christ, he does not belong to Christ" (Rom. 8:9).

Improving Leadership

Hudson Taylor, founder of the China Inland Mission, was a simple yet astute man. He had the gift of saying tremendously significant things in a deceptively simple way. In a letter dated 1879 to the secretary of the mission, Taylor said:

The all-important thing to do is to
1. Improve the character of the work.
2. Deepen the piety, devotion and success of the workers.
3. Remove stones of stumbling, if possible.
4. Oil the wheels where they stick.
5. Amend whatever is defective.
6. Supplement, as far as may be, what is lacking.

Such simple advice reveals insight into a leader's responsibility. An analysis highlights six important areas to care for.

Administration—to improve the character of the work. The leader must discover which departments are functioning below standards and remedy the defect. This may involve developing new job descriptions or establishing new reporting procedures and other lines of communication.

Spiritual tone—to deepen the piety, devotion, and success of the worker. The tone of the church or mission will be a reflection of its leaders. Water rises to the level of its source. The spiritual health of the leadership group should be a top concern among higher echelon leadership. Job satisfaction is also important. If leaders can show their colleagues methods to improve success, their sense of fulfillment will be reflected in an improvement in the quality of their work.

Group morale—to remove stones of stumbling. Friction among a team should be minimized. When problems are neglected, morale drops and performance decreases. If the problem has a remedy, it should be put into place at once. If the problem is a person, the delinquent should be dealt with as soon as the facts are clear, and let the chips fall. Of course the problem or person should be treated with consideration and love, but the work of God cannot be sacrificed for the sake of keeping peace.

Personal relationships—to oil the wheels where they stick. Warm relationships among team members are vital. Some workers prefer to administer; others want to love people. Only the latter are leaders. In handling people, the oil can is much more effective than the acid bottle.

Problem solving—to amend what is defective. One of the chief duties of leaders is to solve tough problems within the organization. Creating problems is easy; solving them is difficult. The leader must face the problem realistically and follow through until the solution is reached.

Creative planning—to supplement what is lacking. Criticizing plans is easier than creating them. The leader must see the goal clearly, plan imaginatively, and employ tactics that lead to success. In this department there is always a short supply of people ready and qualified to perform.

Analyze your leadership responsibilities in light of Hudson Taylor's six points. What are you doing to improve. . .

1. Administration—the character of the work?

2. Spiritual tone—deepening the spiritual health of those who work under you?

3. Group morale—minimizing friction?

4. Personal relationships—building a team?

5. Problem solving—finding solutions?

6. Creative planning—setting goals and employing tactics?

One more way to improve leadership potential: resist the idea of "leadership from the rear." True leadership is always from the top down, never from the bottom up. It was leadership from the rear that led Israel back into the wilderness.

Many churches and organizations are in a stalemate because leaders have submitted to a kind of blackmail from the rear. No dissident or reactionary element should be allowed to determine group policy against the consensus of the spiritual leaders.

---

[1] The reference is to John Bunyan's *Pilgrim's Progress*, published in 1678 and now translated into hundreds of languages. Bunyan (1628–88) wrote more than 60 books.

The Cost of Leadership

Can you drink the cup I drink or be baptized with the baptism I am baptized with?

—Mark 10:38

To aspire to leadership in God's kingdom requires us to be willing to pay a price higher than others are willing to pay. The toll of true leadership is heavy; and the more effective the leadership, the higher it goes.

Quinton Hogg, founder of the London Polytechnic Institute, devoted a fortune to the enterprise. Asked how much it had cost to build the great institution, Hogg replied, "Not very much, simply one man's life blood."[1]

That is the cost of every great achievement, and it is not paid in a lump sum. Achievement is bought on the time-payment plan, with a new installment required each day. Fresh drafts are constantly being drawn, and when payment ceases, leadership wanes. Our Lord taught that we could not save others and ourselves at the same time.

Samuel Brengle wrote:

> Spiritual power is the outpouring of spiritual life, and like all life, from that of the moss and lichen on the wall to that of the archangel before the throne, it is from God. Therefore those who aspire to leadership may pay the price, and seek it from God.[2]

Self-Sacrifice

This part of the cost must be paid daily. A cross stands in the path of spiritual leadership, and the leader must take it up. "Jesus Christ laid down his life for us. And we ought to lay down our lives for our brothers" (1 John 3:16). To the degree the cross of Christ is across our shoulders and over our backs, so the resurrection life of Christ is manifest through us. No cross, no leadership.

"Whoever wants to be first must be slave of all. For even the Son of Man did not come to be served, but to serve, and to give his life as a ransom for many" (Mark 10:44-45). Each of the heroes of faith in Hebrews 11 was called to sacrifice as part of his or her service. Those who lead the church are marked by a willingness to give up personal preferences, to surrender legitimate and natural desires for the sake of God. Bruce Barton quotes a sign at a service station: "We will crawl under your car oftener and get ourselves dirtier than any of our competition."[3] That is the kind of service the Christian seeks to give.

Samuel Zwemer remarked that the only things Jesus took pains to show after His resurrection were His scars.[4] On the Emmaus road His disciples recognized neither Him nor His message. Not until Jesus broke the bread and they possibly saw the scars did they know the person for who He was. When Jesus stood among His demoralized band in the upper room after the resurrection, He showed them both "his hands and [his] side" (John 20:20).

Scars are the authenticating marks of faithful discipleship and true spiritual leadership. It was said of one leader, "He belonged to that class of early martyrs whose passionate soul made an early holocaust of the physical man."[5] Nothing moves people more than the print of the nails and the mark of the spear. Those marks are tests of sincerity that none can challenge, as Paul knew well. "Let no one cause me trouble," he wrote, "for I bear on my body the marks of Jesus" (Gal. 6:17).

How do your "scars" make you a better servant for Jesus?

Hast thou no scar?
No hidden scar on foot, or side, or hand?
I hear thee sung as mighty in the land,
I hear them hail thy bright ascendant star:
Hast thou no scar?

Hast thou no wound?
Yet, I was wounded by the archers, spent.
Leaned me against the tree to die, and rent
By ravening beasts that compassed me, I swooned:
Hast thou no wound?

No wound? No scar?
Yes, as the master shall the servant be,
And pierced are the feet that follow Me;
But thine are whole. Can he have followed far
Who has no wound? No scar?

—Amy Carmichael[6]

Paul described himself and his burden this way: "We are hard pressed on every side, but not crushed; perplexed, but not in despair; persecuted, but not abandoned; struck down, but not destroyed. We always carry around in our body the death of Jesus, so that the life of Jesus may also be revealed in our body. For we who are alive are always being given over to death for Jesus' sake, so that his life may be revealed in our mortal body" (2 Cor. 4:8-11).

Loneliness

Nietzsche believed that life always gets harder toward the summit—the cold gets colder, the wind stronger, the burden of responsibilities heavier.[7]

Because the leader must always be ahead of his followers, he lives with loneliness. Though he may be friendly, there are areas of life where he must walk alone.

> **Describe a time when, as a leader, you felt totally alone.**

Dixon Hoste felt the loneliness when Hudson Taylor retired and placed the leadership of China Inland Mission on his shoulders. Said Hoste after the appointment: "And now I have no one, no one but God!" There he stood on the mount with his God.

We naturally enjoy and need the company of others, and want to share with others the heavy burden of responsibility and care. It is sometimes heartbreaking to make decisions of far-reaching importance that affect the lives of beloved fellow workers—and to make them alone. Moses paid the price for his leadership—alone on the mountain, alone on the plain, misunderstood and criticized.

The Old Testament prophets were lonely men. Enoch walked alone in a decadent society as he preached judgment. His compensation was the presence of God. Jonah was alone in vast Nineveh, a heathen city of a million souls. The loneliest preacher today is the person who has been entrusted with a prophetic message ahead of the times, a message that cuts across the temper of the age.

Gregarious Paul was a lonely man, misunderstood by friends, misrepresented by enemies, deserted by converts. How poignant are his words to Timothy: "You know that everyone in the province of Asia has deserted me" (2 Tim. 1:15).

"Most of the world's greatest souls have been lonely," wrote A. W. Tozer. "Loneliness seems to be the price a saint must pay for his saintliness." The leader must be a person who, while welcoming the friendship and support of all who offer it, has sufficient inner resources to stand alone—even in the face of stiff opposition to have "no one but God."

On without cheer of sister or of daughter,
Yes, without stay of father or of son,
Lone on the land, and homeless on the water,
Pass I in patience till my work be done.

—F. W. H. Meyers

What encourages you when you are facing loneliness?

Fatigue

"The world is run by tired men." Perhaps an overstatement, but there is a grain of reality here. The demands of leadership wear down the most robust person. But Christians know where to find renewal. "Therefore do not lose heart. Though outwardly we are wasting away, yet inwardly we are being renewed day by day" (2 Cor. 4:16). Even Jesus grew weary in ministry and had to rest (John 4:6). Jesus felt depleted in power, inner resources drained, when the needy woman touched His clothing (Mark 5:30). No lasting good can be accomplished without this expenditure of nervous energy and personal power.

The spirit of the welfare state does not produce leaders. If a Christian is not willing to rise early and work late, to expend greater effort in diligent study and faithful work, that person will not change a generation. Fatigue is the price of leadership. Mediocrity is the result of never getting tired.

To the secretary of the Church Missionary Society, Douglas Thornton wrote:

> But I am weary! I have only written because I am too weary to be working now, and too tired to sleep. . . . I am getting prematurely old, they tell me, and doctors do not give me long to live unless the strain is eased a bit. My wife is wearier than I am. She needs complete rest a while. . . . Oh, that the church at home but realized one half of the opportunities of today! Will no one hear the call? Please do your best to help us.[8]

Here were tired missionary leaders grasping the swiftly passing opportunities of their day.

Criticism

"There is nothing else that so kills the efficiency, capability and initiative of a leader as destructive criticism. . . . It tends to hamper and undercut the efficiency of man's thinking process. It chips away at his self-respect and undermines his confidence in his ability to cope with his responsibilities."[9]

No leader lives a day without criticism, and humility will never be more on trial than when criticism comes.

In a letter to a young minister, Fred Mitchell once wrote:

> I am glad to know that you are taking any blessing there may be found in the criticism brought against you by _____, in which case even his bitter attack will yield sweetness. A sentence which has been a great help to Mrs. Mitchell and myself is: "It does not matter what happens to us, but our reaction to what happens to us is of vital importance." I think you must expect more and more criticism, for with increasing responsibility this is inevitable. It causes one to walk humbly with God, and to take such action as He desires.[10]

Samuel Brengle, noted for his sense of holiness, felt the heat of caustic criticism. Instead of rushing to defend himself, he replied: "From my heart I thank you for your rebuke. I think I deserved it. Will you, my friend, remember me in prayer?" When another critic attacked his spiritual life, Brengle replied: "I thank you for your criticism of my life. It set me to self-examination and heart-searching and prayer, which always leads me into a deeper sense of my utter dependence on Jesus for holiness of heart, and into sweeter fellowship with Him."[11]

With such a response, criticism is turned from a curse into a blessing, from a liability into an asset.

How can you turn criticism into a blessing?

Paul sought the favor of God, not of people. His hard work was not to please those around him (Gal. 1:10). Nor was Paul terribly disturbed by criticism. "I care very little if I am judged by you or by any human court. . . . It is the Lord who judges me" (1 Cor. 4:3-4). Paul could afford to take lightly the comments and criticism of others, for his heart was owned by God (Col. 3:22).

Has God ever used criticism in your life to teach you a spiritual lesson?

When?

But link indifference to human opinion with a weak spiritual life, and the result is disaster.

The same independence from human opinion can be a valuable asset to the person whose life goal is the glory of God. Paul's ear was tuned to the voice of God, and human voices were faint by comparison. He was fearless of human judgment, because he was conscious of standing before a higher tribunal (2 Cor. 8:21).

Rejection

The leader who follows high spiritual standards may find himself following his Master on the pathway of rejection, for "he came unto his own and his own received him not."

J. Gregory Mantle tells of a minister whose congregation refused to accept his message. The minister wanted to lead his people into green pastures and beside still waters, but they were unwilling. The ungodly habits of his choir brought things to a head, and the minister invited the choir to resign. That the choir did, and it also persuaded the congregation to remain silent during the singing on the following Sunday. The minister sang alone.

Finally at wit's end, God spoke to him. On a park bench, he saw a piece of torn newspaper, which he picked up to read these words: "No man is ever fully accepted until he has, first of all, been utterly rejected." The minister needed nothing more. He had been utterly rejected for Christ's sake, and his recognition of the fact was the start of a fruitful ministry. Rejected by people, he had been accepted by God.

When, in response to the clear call of God, A. B. Simpson resigned a pastorate, he learned the meaning of "destitute, despised, forsaken." He surrendered a comfortable salary, a position as senior pastor in a great American city, and all claim to denominational help for his yet untried work. He had no following, no organization, no resources, a large family to support, and everyone close to him was predicting failure. He often said that he looked down upon the stone in the street for the sympathy denied him by friends he treasured.

"The rugged path of utter rejection was trodden without complaint, and with rejoicing. He knew that though he . . . was going through fire and water, it was the divinely appointed way to the wealthy place."[12] To such a place Simpson was led. At his death he had established five schools for the training of missionaries, hundreds of missionaries in 16 lands, and many churches in the United States and Canada that exerted a spiritual influence beyond their numbers.

"Often the crowd does not recognize a leader until he has gone, and then they build a monument for him with the stone they threw at him in life."[13]

Pressure and Perplexity

We naively think that the more we grow as Christians, the easier it will be to discern the will of God. But the opposite is often the case. God treats the mature leader as a mature adult, leaving more and more to his or her spiritual discernment and giving fewer bits of tangible guidance than in earlier years. The resulting perplexity adds inevitably to a leader's pressure.

D. E. Hoste said to a friend:

> The pressure! It goes on from stage to stage, [changing] with every period of your life. . . . Hudson Taylor [once] said how in his younger days, things came so clearly, so quickly to him. "But," he said, "now as I have gone on, and God has used me more and more, I seem often to be like a man going along in a fog. I do not know what to do." [14]

But when the time came to act, God always responded to His servant's trust.

People close to a leader pay a price, too. Sometimes a heavier price. Fred Mitchell wrote to his children when he accepted the invitation to become British director of China Inland Mission:

> I have had many a sorrow of heart, and it still remains one of my chief regrets that I have not been able to give myself to mother and you children more. The harvest is great and the labourers few, which means that there have been many calls upon me. I do not justify my negligence, but any sacrifice made by you for our dear Lord Jesus' sake has not been unrewarded. [15]

Is the Holy Spirit leading you to make any response regarding the cost of leadership? If so, what?

[1] Robert E. Speer, *Marks of a Man* (New York: Revell, 1907), 109.

[2] Samuel Logan Brengle, *The Soul-Winner's Secret* (London: Salvation Army, 1918), 23.

[3] The reference is to the famous 1925 book, *The Man Nobody Knows*, written by advertising advocate Bruce Barton. The book purported to show that Jesus was the keenest business mind, and hence the most successful salesman, of all time. Jesus' techniques could revolutionize the world, Barton argued.

[4] Samuel M. Zwemer, *It Is Hard to Be a Christian* (London: Marshalls, 1937), 139. Samuel Marinus Zwemer (1867–1952) established missions to Muslims in the Middle East and was later professor of the history of religion at Princeton Seminary. He wrote more than 50 books.

[5] Lettie Cowman, *Charles E. Cowman* (Los Angeles: Oriental Missionary Society, 1928), 260.

[6] Used by permission of the Christian Literature Crusade, Fort Washington, PA.

[7] Friedrich Nietzsche (1844–1900) was reared Lutheran but as a scholar and university professor of philosophy, he became one of the most well-known atheists of the modern era. In every way he found reason to criticize Christian faith and life, except that he admired Jesus. Nietzsche went insane in 1889 but continued to publish attacks on the church, its mission, and its ethic.

[8] W. H. T. Gairdner, *Douglas M. Thornton* (London: Hodder & Stoughton, n.d.), 225.

[9] R. D. Abella, in *Evangelical Thought* (Manila, n.d.).

[10] Phyllis Thompson, *Climbing on Track* (London: China Inland Mission, 1954), 116.

[11] C. W. Hall, *Samuel Logan Brengle* (New York: Salvation Army, 1933), 272.

[12] J. Gregory Mantle, *Beyond Humiliation* (Chicago: Moody, n.d.), 140–41.

[13] Cowman, 258.

[14] Phyllis Thompson, *D. E. Hoste* (London: China Inland Mission, n.d.), 130–31.

[15] Thompson, *Climbing on Track*, 115.

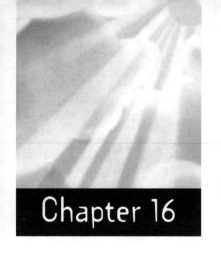

The Responsibilities of Leadership

Besides everything else, I face daily the pressure of my concern for all the churches.
            —2 Corinthians 11:28

Jesus defined leadership as service, and that applies whether a leader works in a secular or a church organization. Field Marshal Montgomery said that his war experience taught him that the staff must be the servant of the troops and that a good staff officer must serve his commander while remaining anonymous himself.

In his book *Training of the Twelve*, A. B. Bruce wrote: "In other kingdoms they rule, whose privilege it is to be ministered unto. In the Divine common-wealth, they rule who account it a privilege to minister."[1] John A. MacKay of Princeton maintained that "servant" is the essential image of the Christian religion. The Son of God became the servant of God in order to do the mission of God. That image provides the pattern for mission societies, churches, and individual believers to fulfill their God-given mission.

The true leader is concerned primarily with the welfare of others, not with his own comfort or prestige. He shows sympathy for the problems of others, but his sympathy fortifies and stimulates; it does not soften and make weak. A spiritual leader will always direct the confidence of others to the Lord. He sees in each emergency a new opportunity for helpfulness. When God chose a leader to succeed Moses, it was Joshua, the man who had proved himself a faithful servant (Ex. 33:11).

D. E. Hoste spoke about the secrets of Hudson Taylor, whom Hoste had followed in leadership of the China Inland Mission:

> Another secret of his influence among us lay in his great sympathy and thoughtful consideration for the welfare and comfort of those about him. The high standard of self-sacrifice and toil which he ever kept before himself, never made him lacking in tenderness and sympathy toward those who were not able to go as far as he did in these respects. He manifested great tenderness and patience toward the failures and shortcomings of his brethren, and was thus able in many cases to help them reach a higher plane of devotion.[2]

Discipline is yet another responsibility of the leader, a duty often unwelcome. Any Christian society requires godly and loving discipline to maintain divine standards in doctrine, morals, and conduct.

Paul describes the spirit required in leaders who exercise discipline. "Brothers, if someone is caught in a sin, you who are spiritual should restore him gently. But watch yourself, or you also may be tempted" (Gal. 6:1). The fundamental ingredient in all discipline is love. "Warn him as a brother" (2 Thess. 3:15). "I urge you, therefore, to reaffirm your love for him" (2 Cor. 2:8). The person who has faced up to his or her own problems and weaknesses is best able to help another in a way both loving and firm. The spirit of meekness will achieve far more than the spirit of criticism.

Approaching a disciplinary situation, the leader must remember five guidelines: (1) First conduct a thorough and impartial inquiry. (2) Then consider the overall benefit to the work and to the individual. (3) Do all in the spirit of love and in the most considerate manner. (4) Always keep the spiritual restoration of the offender in view. (5) Pray it through.

Providing guidance is a third area of responsibility. The spiritual leader must know where he or she is going before presuming to lead others. The leader must go before his flock. The Chief Shepherd gave us the pattern. "When he has brought out all his own, he goes on ahead of them, and his sheep follow him because they know his voice" (John 10:4). "The ideal leader," said A. W. Tozer, "is one who hears the voice of God, and beckons on as the voice calls him and them." Paul gave this challenge to the Corinthian Christians: "Follow my example, as I follow the example of Christ" (1 Cor. 11:1). Paul knew whom he was following and where he was going, and could challenge others to follow him there.

It is not easy to guide people, even mature Christians, who have strong opinions of their own. The leader cannot assert his will recklessly. Said D. E. Hoste:

> In a mission like ours, those guiding its affairs must be prepared to put up with waywardness and opposition, and be able to desist from courses of action which, though they may be intrinsically sound and beneficial, are not approved by some of those affected. Hudson Taylor again and again was obliged either to greatly modify or lay aside projects which were sound and helpful, but met with determined opposition, and so tended to create greater evils than those which might have been removed or mitigated by the changes in question. Later on, in answer to patient continuance in prayer, many of those projects were [put into effect].[3]

A leader must initiate. Some leaders are more gifted at conserving gains than starting new ventures, for maintaining order than generating ardor. The true leader must be venturesome as well as visionary. He must be ready to jump start as well as hold speed. Paul constantly took calculated risks, always carefully and with much prayer, but always reaching for what lay beyond.

The leader must either initiate plans for progress or recognize the worthy plans of others. He must remain in front, giving guidance and direction to those behind. He does not wait for things to happen, but makes them happen. He is a self-starter, always on the lookout for improved methods, eager to test new ideas.

Robert Louis Stevenson called the attitude of safety and security "that dismal fungus."[4] Hudson Taylor took steps of faith that appeared to others as wildcat schemes. The greatest achievements in the history of missions have come from leaders close to God who took courageous, calculated risks.

More failure comes from an excess of caution than from bold experiments with new ideas. A friend who filled an important global post in Christian outreach recently remarked that when he surveyed his life, most of his failures came from insufficient daring. The wife of Archbishop Mowll said, "The frontiers of the kingdom of God were never advanced by men and women of caution."[5]

A leader cannot afford to ignore the counsel of cautious people who can save a mission from mistakes and loss. But caution should not curb vision and initiative, especially when the leader knows God is in control.

To take responsibility willingly is the mark of a leader. Joshua was such a person. He did not hesitate to follow one of the greatest leaders of all history, Moses. Joshua had more reason than Moses to plead inadequacy, but Joshua did not repeat Moses' sin. Instead, he promptly accepted the task he was given and set about the work.

When Elijah was taken up, Elisha did not flinch at stepping in. He accepted the authority conferred by the falling mantle and became a leader in his own right.

In each case these leaders were assured of their divine calling. Once that issue is settled, no one need hesitate to do what God has set before.

Archbishop Benson lived in a different era, but his rules for life carry relevance today:

- Eagerly start the day's main work.
- Do not murmur at your busyness or the shortness of time, but buy up the time all around.
- Never murmur when correspondence is brought in.
- Never exaggerate duties by seeming to suffer under the load, but treat all responsibilities as liberty and gladness.
- Never call attention to crowded work or trivial experiences.
- Before confrontation or censure, obtain from God a real love for the one at fault. Know the facts; be generous in your judgment. Otherwise, how ineffective, how unintelligible or perhaps provocative your well-intentioned censure may be.
- Do not believe everything you hear; do not spread gossip.
- Do not seek praise, gratitude, respect, or regard for past service.
- Avoid complaining when your advice or opinion is not consulted, or having been consulted, set aside.
- Never allow yourself to be placed in favorable contrast with anyone.
- Do not press conversation to your own needs and concerns.
- Seek no favors, nor sympathies; do not ask for tenderness, but receive what comes.
- Bear the blame; do not share or transfer it.
- Give thanks when credit for your own work or ideas is given to another.[6]

Complete this list of responsibilities a leader must accept.

1. Being primarily concerned with the _____.

2. _____ to maintain divine standards.

3. Providing _____.

4. Be visionary and _____ new plans.

5. Take _____ willingly.

Reread Archbishop Benson's rules for life and put a star beside any rule you need to put into practice.

---

[1] Alexander Balmain Bruce (1831–99) was professor of apologetics and New Testament at the Free Church College, Glasgow, from 1868 to1899. He wrote *Training of the Twelve* in 1871.

[2] Phyllis Thompson, *D. E. Hoste* (London: China Inland Mission, n.d.), 217.

[3] Ibid., 158.

[4] In *The Reaper*, May 1961, 89. Robert Louis Stevenson (1850–94) was a British writer best known for *Treasure Island* and *Dr. Jekyll and Mr. Hyde*.

[5] Marcus Loane, *Archbishop Mowll* (London: Hodder & Stoughton, 1960), 249.

[6] From *The Life of Robert E. Speer*. The text as it appeared in that work has been paraphrased. Edward White Benson (1829–96) became archbishop of Canterbury in 1882. His leadership of the Church of England was marked by concerns for education and the church in Wales.

Tests of Leadership

God tested Abraham.
—Genesis 22:1

Then Jesus was led by the Spirit into the desert to be tempted by the devil.
—Matthew 4:1

To everyone entrusted with spiritual authority, searching tests are bound to come.

Let Go Your Desires -Self

Discipline -focus-Self

Brokenness Willing Self

My Desires vs Gods. Desires

Compromise

Can we waive a principle to reach agreement? Lowering standards is always a backward step, and compromise nearly always requires it.

The epic contest of Moses and Pharaoh is a classic example of the temptation to compromise. When Pharaoh realized that Moses meant to lead the Hebrews out of Egypt, he used cunning and threats to frustrate him. "Worship God if you will," was his first overture, "but don't leave Egypt to do it." A modern equivalent would be: "Religion is okay, but don't be narrow about it. No need to let religion isolate you from the rest of the world."

When that approach failed, Pharaoh tried something else: "If you must go out of Egypt to worship, don't go far. Religion is fine, but there is no need to be fanatical about it. Stay as close to the world as you can."

Yet a third attempt played on natural affection: "Let the men go and worship, and the women and children stay here. If you must break with the world, don't force such a narrow lifestyle on everyone else in the family."

Pharaoh's last attempt was an appeal to greed: "Okay, go. But the flocks and herds stay. Don't let your odd religious commitments get in the way of business and prosperity."

With clear spiritual insight Moses cut through each evasion: "Not a hoof is to be left behind," he said (Ex. 10:26). So Moses passed with honors a great test of his leadership of God's people.

Ambition

All great leaders—Moses, too—face this test. During Moses' absence on Mount Sinai, the people of Israel turned to idolatry; and God became very angry, saying, "I will strike them down with a plague and destroy them, but I will make you into a nation greater and stronger than they" (Num. 14:12).

Already Moses had heard more than enough of the peoples' constant complaining and frequent dalliance with paganism. Why not accept this divine proposal as a way to give the people their due, and start afresh with a smaller group that Moses could certainly control?

What a test, from the mouth of God Himself. Instead of personal ambition, Moses showed selfless nobility, genuine concern for God's glory, and compassion for the misguided people. Not for a moment did the thought of self-aggrandizement enter his lofty mind. He held on to God audaciously and tenaciously. Through prayer, Moses saved the apostate nation from judgment.

The Impossible Situation

"How does this person face impossible situations?" John R. Mott would inquire as a way to separate leaders from followers. Mott encouraged leaders to deal with impossible tasks rather than easy ones in order to foster personal competence, teamwork, and faith. "I long since ceased to occupy myself with minor things that can be done by others," he said. A true leader rises to face baffling circumstances and complex problems.

Our own day presents leaders with difficult problems as never before. If leaders are to survive, they must view the difficult as commonplace, the complex as normal.

Moses faced an impossible situation when Israel reached the Red Sea. On one side was the desert and Pharaoh's army; on the other side was water, and Israel had no boats. Moses was in a cul-de-sac, and the people were getting edgy. Complaints started flying as morale dropped: "Is it because there were no graves in Egypt that you have taken us away to die in the wilderness?"

Moses, great man of faith, stayed himself on God. His order must have sounded like sheer fantasy, but in point of fact it was a defining moment of his leadership.

"Do not fear!" he cried, against every good reason to fear.

"Stand by!" he cried, as Pharaoh sped toward them.

"See the salvation of the Lord!"

So on that strange and wonderful day the people of Israel saw their God in action, their hopes affirmed, their enemies crushed. The bracing lesson is that God delights to lead people, and then, in response to their trust, to show them power that matches every impossible situation.

Hudson Taylor faced many hard situations in his career to win China for Christ. He counted three phases in most great tasks undertaken for God—impossible, difficult, *done*.

> Have you come to the Red Sea place in your life,
> Where in spite of all you can do,
> There is no way out, there is no way back,
> There is no other way but through?
> Then wait on the Lord with a trust serene
> Till the night of your fear is gone;
> He will send the wind, He will heap the floods,
> When He says to your soul, "Go on."

In the morning watch, 'neath the lifted cloud,
You shall see but the Lord alone,
When He leads you on from the place of the sea
To a land that you have not known;
And your fears shall pass as your foes have passed,
You shall no more be afraid;
You shall sing His praise in a better place,
A place that His hand has made.

—Annie Johnson Flint [1]

Failure

Many people who appear to be at the height of their careers hide a great inner sense of failure. Alexander Maclaren, the great British preacher, delivered a wonderful address to a large crowd, but turned away, overwhelmed with failure. "I must not speak on such an occasion again," he said, while the congregation went away blessed and inspired.[2]

Were his expectations too high? Or did the devil bring him grief when he should have felt great joy?

How a leader handles failure will set much of the agenda for the future. Peter appeared washed up as a leader after his denial of the Christ; but repentance and love reopened the door of opportunity, and Peter's leadership touched all the rest of Christendom. "Where sin abounded, grace did much more abound."

Most Bible characters met with failure and survived. Even when the failure was immense, those who found leadership again refused to lie in the dust and bemoan their tragedy. In fact, their failure and repentance led to a greater conception of God's grace. They came to know the God of the second chance, and sometimes the third and fourth.

The historian Froude wrote: "The worth of a man must be measured by his life, not by his failure under a singular and peculiar trial. Peter the apostle, though forewarned, [three times] denied the Master on the first alarm of danger; yet that Master, who knew his nature in its strength and in its [weakness], chose him."[3]

Successful leaders have learned that no failure need be final, whether his own failure or someone else's. No one is perfect, and we cannot be right all the time.

Jealousy

Most leaders at some time face the problem of a jealous rival. Even Moses encountered that test. Jealousy is a common weapon of the devil.

Moses' first such challenge came from within his own family—his sister and brother. They had apparently forgotten that without Moses' self-abnegating response to the divine call to lead the people out of Egypt, they and all the rest of Israel would still be living under the slavemaster's lash.

Miriam by this time was an elderly woman, and her experience of God should have taught her the evil and ugliness of jealousy. She promoted gossip against Moses because of his marriage to an Ethiopian. Race hatred is not the sin of the 20th century alone. Miriam resented the intrusion of a foreigner and drew the weakling Aaron into her rebellion.

Not content with second place, Miriam and Aaron, led by the devil, tried to remove Moses by a coup. They cloaked their treachery in piety: "Has the Lord spoken only by Moses? Has He not also spoken by us?"

Moses was deeply wounded, but he said nothing to vindicate himself. His main concern was God's glory, not his own position or privilege. "Now Moses was a very humble man, more humble than anyone else on the face of the earth" (Num. 12:3). Yet though Moses maintained a dignified silence, God would not allow such a challenge to the authority of His servant to go without response.

Because the offense was public, judgment and punishment would also be public. "When the cloud lifted from above the Tent, there stood Miriam— leprous, like snow," the record runs (Num. 12:10). Such a drastic punishment points to the gravity of her sin; and once again Moses' greatness shines. His only response was to pray for his sister, and God graciously responded in mercy.

The lesson for the leader is plain. The person who fills a role appointed by God need not worry about vindicating his or her work when rivals become jealous or treacherous. Such a leader is safe in the hands of a heavenly Protector. Indeed, God shows how safe with His ominous words to Miriam: "Why then were you not afraid to speak against my servant Moses?" (Num. 12:8).

Moses faced a second challenge from Korah and his henchmen, noted for their jealousy of Moses and Aaron. Korah wondered why these special two should enjoy the privilege of high office. Were not others (himself for one) equally deserving and qualified?

Once again Moses refused to vindicate himself against their charges. God intervened, judgment was rendered, and Moses stood higher than ever while the people grew in fear of God.

God will defend the leaders He has chosen. He will honor, protect, and vindicate them. Leaders need not worry about defending their rights or their office.

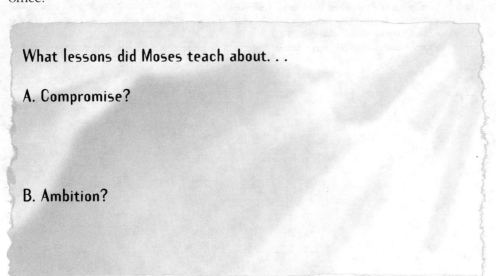

What lessons did Moses teach about. . .

A. Compromise?

B. Ambition?

C. The Impossible Situation?

D. Jealousy?

What does the life of Peter teach about handling failure?

If you were giving advice to young ministers, how would you tell them to face situations that test their leadership and call?

---

[1] Used by permission of Evangelical Publishers, Toronto, Canada.

[2] Alexander Maclaren (1826–1910) was pastor for 45 years at Union Chapel in Manchester, England. He was first president of the Baptist World Alliance in 1905.

[3] James Anthony Froude (1818–94) was a British writer and historian attached to the Oxford Movement.

The Art of Delegation

*He chose capable men from all Israel and made them leaders of the people. . . .
They served as judges for the people at all times. The difficult cases they brought
to Moses.*

       —Exodus 18:25-26

One facet of leadership is the ability to recognize the special abilities and
limitations of others, combined with the capacity to fit each one into the job
where he or she will do best. To succeed in getting things done through others
is the highest type of leadership. Dwight L. Moody, a shrewd judge of people,
once said that he would rather put a thousand men to work than do the work
of a thousand men.[1] D. E. Hoste said: "The capacity to appreciate the gifts of
widely varying kinds of workers, and then to help them along the lines of their
own personalities and workings, is the main quality for oversight in a mission
such as ours."[2]

Thoughtful delegation will save the leader the frustrating experience of
square pegs serving in round holes.

Delegation to others of responsibility, together with the authority to do the
job, is not always relished by one who enjoys exercising the authority himself.
He is glad to give the responsibility to others but reluctant to let the reins of
power slip from his own hands. Also, some leaders feel threatened by brilliant
subordinates and, therefore, are reluctant to delegate authority. Whatever the
basic cause, failure to delegate authority is unfair to the subordinate and unlike-
ly to prove satisfactory or effective. Such an attitude tends to be interpreted as
indicating a lack of confidence, and that does not promote the best cooperation;
neither will it draw out the full abilities of the one being trained for leadership.

It is possible that the subordinate may not do the task as well as his
superior, but experience proves that that is by no means necessarily the case.
Given the chance, the younger person may do it better because he or she is
better able to feel the pulse of contemporary life. But in any case, how is the
younger leader to gain experience unless he or she has been delegated both
the responsibility and the authority for the task?

The degree to which a leader is able to delegate work is a measure of his
success. A one-person office can never grow larger than the load one person
can carry.

Failing to delegate, the leader is caught in a morass of secondary detail; it overburdens him and diverts his attention from primary tasks. People under him do not achieve their own potential. In some cases, insisting on doing a job one-self is a result of simple conceit.

Once a leader delegates, he should show utmost confidence in the people he has entrusted. A. B. Simpson trusted those in charge of the various schools he founded, leaving them free to exercise their own gifts.[3] If they failed, Simpson took it as a reflection of his own failed leadership, for he had selected them.

Subordinates perform better when they feel sure of the leader's support, whether a given project succeeds or fails, so long as they have acted within the bounds of their assignment. This confidence comes when responsibilities have been clearly defined in writing, to eliminate any misunderstandings. Failing to communicate clearly has led to many unhappy problems.

Paul Super wrote of his association with John R. Mott:

> One of my greatest resources these ten years in Poland is the sense
> of his backing. My greatest pride is his belief in me. Surely one of
> my greatest motives is to be worthy of his support and to measure
> up to his expectations of me.[4]

One of the great biblical illustrations of this principle is the story of Jethro, father-in-law to Moses, recorded in Exodus 18. Israel emerged from Egypt an unorganized horde of ex-slaves. By the time of Exodus 18, a new national spirit was developing. Jethro saw that Moses faced intolerably heavy burdens—he was dealing with problems from morning till night. Moses was the legislature; Moses was the judiciary; Moses was the executive branch of the new nation. His decisions were accepted by the people as God's will.

Jethro saw that Moses could not keep up such a pace and made two solid arguments for delegating some of the work. First, "you and these people who come to you will only wear yourselves out. The work is too heavy for you; you cannot handle it alone" (Ex. 18:18). Moses was at his limit, probably beyond his limit, of physical and emotional resources. Second, the current method of problem solving was too slow, and people were getting impatient. Sharing authority would speed up legal action, and the people would go away satisfied (18:23).

Then Jethro proposed a two-part plan. Moses would continue to teach spiritual principles and exercise legislative leadership. He also would decide the hard cases at court. But much of his work would be delegated to competent, trustworthy subordinates.

Jethro spoke wisely, for if Moses had succumbed under the strain, he would have left chaos behind—no one trained to lead, no one in charge of anything. Failure to make provision for the succession of leadership has spelled ruin for many missions and churches.

Moses followed Jethro's advice and realized several benefits. He was able to concentrate on the biggest problems. The latent talents of many around him were discovered. Those gifted men, who could have become his critics had Moses continued alone, were now allies facing a common challenge. People-problems were solved with efficiency. And Moses laid the groundwork for effective leadership after his death.

Jethro encouraged Moses by articulating a spiritual principle of timeless relevance. "If you do this and God so commands, you will be able to stand the strain" (18:23). Jethro placed his advice under the authority of God. God takes all responsibility for enabling His servants to do their work. Some tasks others can do better, and those should be delegated. But even if those secondary tasks are not done perfectly, still delegation is the better part of wisdom. Moses was probably better at judging than any of the 70 associate judges he appointed; but had he persisted alone, his career would have been cut short.

Jethro's spiritual discernment comes through in the qualifications he puts forward for the selection of this cadre: men of ability, for their work is formidable; men of piety, for fear of God is the beginning of wisdom; men of honor, who would shun bribes and greed.

It is a big mistake to assume more duties than we can discharge. There is no virtue in doing more than our fair share of the work. We do well to recognize our limitations. Our Jethros can often discern better than we can the impact of all our duties, and we should listen to them. If we break natural law—humans must sleep as well as work, for example—we cannot be exempt from repercussions. If we succumb to human persuasion and take on more than we should, God will accept no responsibility for the outcome.

Missionary leadership must be ready to delegate responsibility to nationals the moment they give evidence of spiritual maturity. Then the missionary must stand by them, ready to help but reluctant to intervene, guiding the national through trial and error so that he or she might learn spiritual leadership as the missionary did. Delegating in this way fulfills the essential task of discovering, training, and using the latent talents of national Christian colleagues. In the earlier stages, a wise watchfulness is necessary; but interfering should be reserved for acute needs only. The sense of being watched destroys confidence.

When W. E. Sangster was appointed general secretary of the Home Mission Department of the Methodist Church in Britain, he divided labor between his subordinates, assigned each responsibilities, and gave up all supervision. He never regretted placing such trust. It was said of Sangster: "Perhaps his greatest grasp of leadership was knowing the importance of delegation and of choosing assistants with care. He was always a master of that art."[5]

Writing about the leader of a large missionary society, a member of his staff commented: "He had a great gift of leadership in that he never interfered with those who worked under him. Everyone was left to do his own work." Another member wrote, "He knew what people could do, and saw that they did it, leaving them to make the best of their opportunities, and investigating only if things went wrong."[6]

> **Summarize the leadership lessons one can learn from Moses and Jethro in Exodus 18.**

Evaluate your own ability to delegate by answering these questions:

1. How easy is it for you to assign others a responsible task?

2. Once delegated, how do you hold the person accountable for the task?

3. When delegating work, how do you encourage and support the person you have entrusted?

4. How do you feel if the person does the work better than you could do it?

Is the Holy Spirit guiding you to make any changes in your delegation or responsibilities to others? _____

If so, what steps will you take to get more things done through others?

---

[1] Dwight Lyman Moody (1837–99) was one of America's foremost evangelists. He rose to national prominence after success in preaching meetings in Scotland and England during 1873–75. He established educational institutions in Northfield, Massachusetts, and Chicago (later called Moody Bible Institute).

[2] Phyllis Thompson, *D. E. Hoste* (London: China Inland Mission, n.d.), 56.

[3] A. E. Thompson, *The Life of A. B. Simpson* (Harrisburg, PA: Christian Publications, 1920), 208.

[4] B. Matthews, *John R. Mott* (London: Hodder & Stoughton, 1909), 364.

[5] Paul E. Sangster, *Doctor Sangster* (London: Epworth, 1962), 88, 221.

[6] Phyllis Thompson, *Climbing on Track* (London: China Inland Mission, 1954), 99.

Replacing Leaders

Moses my servant is dead. Now then, you and all these people, get ready to cross the Jordan River into the land I am about to give to them. . . . As I was with Moses, so I will be with you.

—Joshua 1:2, 5

The true test of a person's leadership is the health of the organization when the organizer is gone. This truth was behind Gamaliel's counsel to fellow Pharisees: "Leave these men alone! Let them go! For if their purpose or activity is of human origin, it will fail. But if it is from God, you will not be able to stop these men" (Acts 5:38–39). A work inspired by God and built on spiritual principles will survive the shock of leadership change and may even prosper as a result.

We sometimes demean God by thinking that the death of a great leader takes God by surprise or sends God into emergency action. Though we may feel shock and anxiety, we must remember that Christian leadership is different from the worldly sort. God selects and prepares leaders for the kingdom (Mark 10:40). No work of God will be left destitute until its purposes are achieved.

Great movements are often thrown into crisis at the death of a founder. Such crises need not be fatal, however. Lyman Beecher said that he despaired when the first secretary of the American Board of Missions died. Then another leader arose and did so well that Beecher felt despair again when the second secretary died. At last, when the third secretary proved himself competent, Beecher began to feel confident that God's resources were equal to the task at hand. When Beecher himself was gone, some believed he could not be replaced. But all of Beecher's causes—temperance, orthodoxy, and foreign missions—found capable new leaders in God's time and way.[1] Indeed, no man, however gifted and devoted, is indispensable to the work of the kingdom.

God is always at work, though we cannot see it, preparing people He has chosen for leadership. When the crisis comes, God fits His appointee into the place ordained for him. Often such a replacement is not apparent to an organization, but time will reveal him.

> **What does a wise spiritual leader realize about himself and the leaders in his ministry?**

God's greatest gifts to Israel, better than the land itself, were men such as Moses and David and Isaiah. His greatest endowment to the church was the gift of twelve men trained for leadership.

Imagine how distraught the Israelites were when the time approached for Moses to leave them. For four decades the entire nation had looked to Moses for problem solving and direction. Moses had interpreted the will of God for them. True, 70 elders served under him, but there was not another Moses. Adding to the sense of crisis was the timing of his death, just at the point of entry in Canaan. The people could hardly believe that God had a new leader in reserve. But Joshua was in preparation, and the crisis brought him to the fore.

This situation is repeated throughout history; each generation learns the same lesson. The loss of an outstanding leader awakens doubts and fears. What will the Methodists do without Wesley? What will the Salvation Army do without Booth? What will our church do when the pastor moves?

The paths of glory lead always to the grave, but a new glory will be revealed. The greatest leader must inevitably be removed by death or some other cause, and the sense of loss will vary with the caliber of his leadership. But in retrospect it will usually be seen that the seeming tragedy has actually turned out to be in the best interests of the work.

Only after his removal are the character and achievements of a leader fully revealed. It was not until after Moses' death that Israel saw his greatness in its true perspective. "The emphasis of death makes perfect the lessons of the life."

At the same time, a leader's passing cuts his persona down to size in relation to the work of God. The time comes when his special contribution is not the need of the hour. The most gifted leader has liabilities and limitations that become apparent when a successor comes along to advance the work. Often a successor with less fame and prestige than a founder is better able to develop the work because of the specific gifts he has. We must assume that Joshua was better equipped to conquer Canaan than Moses.

Often when the weight of responsibility falls suddenly upon his shoulders, a subordinate develops abilities and qualities he and others had not suspected he had. Joshua never would have developed into an outstanding leader had he remained one of Moses' lieutenants.

A shift in leadership also provides occasion for God to show His versatility in adjusting means to ends. His resources in any work He initiates are inexhaustible. If a man who possesses great gifts will not place them at the disposal of God, He is not defeated. He will take a man of lesser gifts that are fully available to Him and will supplement those gifts with His own mighty power.

Identify some positive outcomes when there is a change in leadership. ✓

Paul implied this when he wrote to the Corinthians in 1 Corinthians 1:26-29:

> Brothers, think of what you were when you were called. Not many of you were wise by human standards; not many were influential; not many were of noble birth. But God chose the foolish things of the world to shame the wise; God chose the weak things of the world to shame the strong. He chose the lowly things of this world and the despised things—and the things that are not—to nullify the things that are, so that no one may boast before him.

God is surely eager to use the powers of naturally gifted people, but few of them are as willing as was Paul to place those gifts without reservation at God's disposal. When such people learn to rely not on their own power and wisdom, but to depend on God, there is no limit to their usefulness in God's service.

Toward the end of his life, A. B. Simpson was at a great convention when a respected New York minister observed that there was no one similarly qualified to continue leadership of the organization when Simpson's tenure was done. The minister suggested that a large endowment be established to ensure that the work continue. Simpson said nothing and did nothing. He believed that if his work was from God, nothing could dismantle it; if it were not from God, no good purpose was served by keeping it going.[2]

How Simpson rejoiced during the last months of his life, when he had retired from leadership in the Alliance, as reports came in of increased missionary offerings and progress on the foreign fields. The year after his death proved to be the most prosperous year in the history of the society. No greater tribute could be paid to the quality of Simpson's leadership.

Only one Leader holds office forever; no successor is needed for Him. The disciples made no move to appoint a replacement for Jesus, tacit evidence that they were conscious of His abiding presence, their living leader and Lord. At times the church has lost a vivid sense of Jesus' presence, but there has never been the panic cry of a leaderless army. The perils and distress of the church weigh deeply on Jesus' heart.

Since our Leader conducts His work in the power of an endless life—He is the same yesterday, today, and forever—changes in human leadership should not shake or dismay us.

Why is it important to remember that the True Leader of the church holds office forever?

---

[1] *Sunday School Times*, 8 November 1913, 682. Lyman Beecher (1775–1863) was one of America's leading revival preachers, New England pastor, and president of Lane Seminary.

[2] A. E. Thompson, *The Life of A. B. Simpson* (Harrisburg, PA.: Christian Publications, 1920), 208.

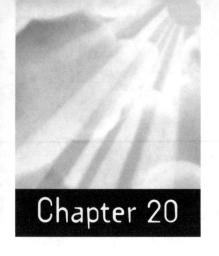

Reproducing Leaders

The things you have heard me say in the presence of many witnesses entrust to reliable men who will also be qualified to teach others.

—2 Timothy 2:2

With these words Paul presses home a leader's responsibility to train others to lead.

> **What steps do you take to train those under you to take leadership positions?**

If he is to carry out his trust fully, the leader will devote time to training others to succeed and perhaps even supersede him. Barnabas's spiritual stature is seen in his entire freedom from jealousy when his protégé Paul surpassed his own leadership skills and became the dominant member of the team. It follows that a leader must provide subordinates with opportunity to exercise and develop their powers.

John R. Mott believed that leaders must multiply themselves by developing younger leaders, giving them full play and adequate outlet for their abilities. Younger people should feel the weight of heavy burdens, opportunity for initiative, and power of final decision. The younger leader should receive generous credit for achievements. Foremost, he must be trusted. Blunders are the inevitable price of training leaders.

At a recent missionary conference, an Asian leader spoke frankly about the role of Western missionaries: "The missionary of today in the Orient should be less a performer, and more a trainer." This may not be true in every missionary setting, but it does highlight one of the great needs in current mission strategy.

Training new leaders is a delicate task. The wise trainer will not advertise the end he has in view. Bishop Stephen Neill spoke of the danger of this task:

If we set out to produce a race of leaders, what we shall succeed in doing is probably to produce a race of restless, ambitious and discontented intellectuals. To tell a man he is called to be a leader is the best way of ensuring his spiritual ruin, since in the Christian world ambition is more deadly than any other sin, and, if yielded to, makes a man unprofitable in the ministry. The most important thing today is the spiritual, rather than the intellectual, quality of those indigenous Christians who are called to bear responsibility in the younger churches.

Lesslie Newbigin goes so far as to question whether the church ought to encourage the concept of leadership, so difficult it is to use without being misled by its non-Christian counterpart. The church needs saints and servants, not "leaders"; and if we forget the priority of service, the entire idea of leadership training becomes dangerous. Leadership training must still follow the pattern our Lord used with His twelve.[1]

spiritual ? human ? training

> **Explain the relevance of this quote: "The church needs saints and servants, not 'leaders,' and if we forget the priority of service, the entire idea of leadership training becomes dangerous."**

Perhaps the most strategic and fruitful work of modern missionaries is to help leaders of tomorrow develop their spiritual potential. This task requires careful thought, wise planning, endless patience, and genuine Christian love. It cannot be haphazard or ill-conceived. Our Lord devoted the greater part of His three years of ministry to molding the characters and spirits of His disciples.

> **What can you learn from Jesus' leadership training style?** ✓

✗ compassion
✗ explanation in their terms
✗ patience
✗ love for all + included

Paul showed the same concern for training young Timothy and Titus. Paul's method for preparing Timothy for the church in Ephesus is deeply instructive.

Timothy was about 20 years old when Paul became his friend. Timothy tended toward melancholia, and he was too tolerant of and partial to people of rank. He could be irritable with opponents. He was apt to rely on old spiritual experiences rather than kindle the flame of daily devotion.

But Paul had high hopes for him. Paul set about to correct Timothy's timid nature, to replace softness with steel. Paul led Timothy into experiences and hardships that toughened his character. Paul did not hesitate to assign him tasks beyond his present powers. How else can a young person develop competence and confidence if not by stretching to try the impossible?[2]

Traveling with Paul brought Timothy into contact with men of stature whose characters kindled in him a wholesome ambition. From his mentor he learned to meet triumphantly the crises that Paul considered routine. Paul shared with Timothy the work of preaching. Paul gave him the responsibility of establishing a group of Christians at Thessalonica. Paul's exacting standards, high expectations, and heavy demands brought out the best in Timothy, saving him from a life of mediocrity.

Paul Rees describes the experience of Douglas Hyde, one-time Communist but later a convert to Christ, as recorded in Hyde's book, *Dedication and Leadership Techniques*:

> Easily one of the most fascinating stories in the book—a story connected with his Communist years—involves a young man who came to Douglas Hyde and announced that he wanted to be made into a leader. "I thought," said Hyde, "I had never seen anyone look less like a leader in my life. He was short, grotesquely fat, with a great, flabby, wide uninteresting face. . . . He had a cast in one eye, and spoke with a most distressing stutter."
>
> What happened? Well, instead of turning him away as a hopeless prospect, Hyde gave him a chance to study, to learn, to test his dedication, to smooth out his stutter. In the end he became a leader in one of the most Communist-infiltrated labour unions in Britain.[3]

The observant leader may discover latent talent in some quite unpromising people.

Frank Buchman, founder of Moral Rearmament, displayed many leadership gifts. He claimed that if he failed to train others to do his work better than he did it, he had failed. For many years he worked to make himself dispensable, a rare agenda for a founder.[4]

No work is more rewarding to a missionary than developing leaders, for the development of the new churches the missionary founds will greatly depend on the spiritual caliber of the national Christians. Once the pioneer stage in any field has passed, the training of leadership should take high priority. One of a missionary's main goals should be the development of faith in promising young people who can, in time, lead the church.

Lest our training programs become too rigid and we discourage the exceptional person from service, we must always allow room for the unusual person, the one for whom there is no mold. God has His "irregulars," and many of them have made outstanding contributions to world evangelization. Who could have poured C. T. Studd into a mold? Such men and women cannot be measured by ordinary standards or made to conform to any fixed pattern.

One such missionary was Douglas Thornton, who made an indelible mark among Muslims in the Near East. He possessed rare gifts, and even as a young man did not hesitate to express opinions that seemed radical and impractical to his superiors. His biographer records:

> It is hardly surprising to learn that he felt constrained to write to his society a memorandum setting forth his views on the past, present and future of the work in Egypt. It is not a precedent that young missionaries after three and a half months on the field should be invited to follow, and on this occasion, too, heads were shaken. But Thornton was an exceptional man, and time has proved that his views and even his effusions were worthy of being studied. It was never safe to neglect them. Most juniors had best reserve their observations for a more mature season. But when the exceptional man arrives, two things have to be observed—the man has to learn to make his observations in the right way, so as to carry his seniors with him; the seniors have to learn how to learn from one who is possibly able, in spite of his want of local knowledge, to benefit them enormously by his fresh and spontaneous ideas. Each is a difficult lesson.[5]

Leadership training cannot be done on a mass scale. It requires patient, careful instruction and prayerful, personal guidance over a considerable time. "Disciples are not manufactured wholesale. They are produced one by one, because someone has taken the pains to discipline, to instruct and enlighten, to nurture and train one that is younger."

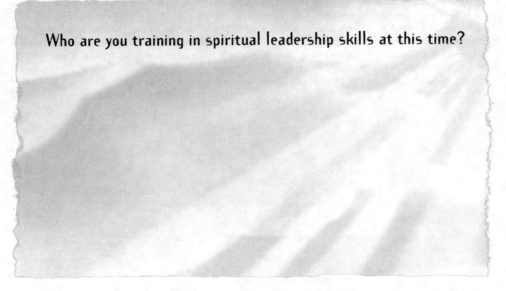

Who are you training in spiritual leadership skills at this time?

When a person is really marked out for leadership, God will see that that person receives the necessary disciplines for effective service.

When God wants to drill a man
 And thrill a man
 And skill a man,
When God wants to mold a man
 To play the noblest part;
When He yearns with all His heart
 To create so great and bold a man
That all the world shall be amazed,
 Watch His methods, watch His ways!
How He ruthlessly perfects
 Whom He royally elects!
How He hammers him and hurts him,
 And with mighty blows converts him
Into trial shapes of clay which
 Only God understands;
While his tortured heart is crying
 And he lifts beseeching hands!
How He bends but never breaks
 When his good He undertakes;
How He uses whom He chooses
 And with every purpose fuses him;
 By every act induces him
To try His splendour out.
 God knows what He's about!
                    —Author unknown

---

[1] Lesslie Newbigin, in *International Review of Missions*, April 1950. Newbigin retired after 40 years of missionary service in India.

[2] H. C. Lees, *St. Paul's Friends* (London: Religious Tract Society, 1917), 135–41.

[3] Paul S. Rees, "The Community Clue," *Life of Faith,* 26 September 1976, 3.

[4] P. Howard, *Frank Buchman* (London: Heineman, 1961), 111. Frank Nathan Daniel Buchman (1878–1961) was a Lutheran minister who, discouraged with his work, moved to England in 1908. There he came in contact with the Keswick movement and experienced a conversion. In 1938 he launched the Moral Rearmament movement to promote love, honesty, purity, and unselfishness. The movement endured criticism from conservative Christians for alleged humanism. In Sanders's first edition, he makes a point of not endorsing "the merits" of Buchman's movement.

[5] W. H. T. Gairdner, *Douglas M. Thornton* (London: Hodder & Stoughton, n.d.), 121.

Perils of Leadership

So that after I have preached to others, I myself will not be disqualified for the prize.

     —1 Corinthians 9:27

The perils of spiritual leadership are especially subtle, more so than for other callings. The leader is not immune from temptations of the flesh, but the greater dangers are in the realm of spirit, for the enemy Satan never fails to exploit the advantage in any area of weakness.

Pride

When a person rises in position, as happens to leaders in the church, the tendency to pride also increases. If not checked, the attitude will disqualify the person from further advancement in the kingdom of God, for "the LORD detests all the proud of heart" (Prov. 16:5). These are strong and searching words! Nothing aggravates God more than conceit, the sin that aims at setting the self upon a throne, making of God a secondary figure. That very sin changed the anointed cherub into the foul fiend of hell.

Pride takes many forms, but spiritual pride is the most grievous. To become proud of spiritual gifts or leadership position is to forget that all we have is from God, all the position we occupy is by God's appointment.

The victim of pride is often least aware of the sin. Three tests help us identify the problem:

The test of precedence.—How do we react when another is selected for the position we expected to have or wanted to fill? when another is promoted in our place? when another's gifts seem greater than our own?

The test of sincerity.—In our moments of honest self-reflection, we often admit to problems and weaknesses. How do we feel when others identify the same problems in us?

The test of criticism.—Does criticism lead to immediate resentment and self-justification? Do we rush to criticize the critic?

If we are honest, when we measure ourselves by the life of Jesus, who humbled Himself on the cross, we are overwhelmed with the shabbiness, even the vileness, of our hearts, and we cry:

        Boasting excluded, pride I abase;
        I'm only a sinner, saved by grace.

                —James M. Gray

Name the three tests for spiritual pride:

1.

2.

3.

Who is the best standard of measurement?

Egotism

One of the repulsive manifestations of pride, egotism is the practice of thinking and speaking of oneself, of magnifying one's attainments and relating everything to the self rather than to God and God's people. The leader who has long enjoyed the admiration of many followers stands in peril of this danger.

When Robert Louis Stevenson arrived in Samoa, he was invited to address students training for the pastorate at the Malua Institute. His talk was based on the Muslim story of the veiled prophet, a brilliant teacher who wore a veil because, he claimed, the glory of his presence was too great for men to bear the sight.

At last the veil grew ragged and fell off. Then the people discovered that the brilliant prophet was only a decrepit old man trying to hide his ugliness. Stevenson went on to make the point that, however grand the truths a preacher taught, however skillfully he might excuse blemishes of character, the time comes when the veil falls away and a man is seen by the people as he really is. Will the leader reflect the ugliness of egotism or the transfigured glory of Christ the Lord?

> It is a good test to the rise and fall of egotism to notice how you listen to the praises of other men of your own standing. Until you can listen to the praises of a rival without any desire to indulge in detraction or any attempt to belittle his work, you may be sure there is an unmortified prairie of egotistic impulse in your nature yet to be brought under the grace of God.[1]

Jealousy

This near relative of pride describes the person who is suspicious of rivals. Moses faced such a temptation through the loyalty of his own colleagues. "Eldad and Medad are prophesying in the camp," a young man reported. An outraged Joshua exclaimed, "Moses, my lord, stop them!" (Num. 11:27-28).

But the great leader saw the situation for what it was: an outbreak of God's Spirit among the assistants Moses had selected. "Are you jealous for my sake?" Moses replied to Joshua. "I wish that all the LORD's people were prophets" (Num. 11:29). Envy and jealousy found no fertile ground in Moses' heart. God's work in others was to be encouraged, not snuffed out.

Popularity

What leader or preacher does not desire to be liked by his people? Being disliked is no virtue, but popularity can have too high a price. "Woe unto you when all men speak well of you," Jesus warned.

Personality cults have often developed around great spiritual leaders. Followers are awestruck at a leader's virtues, and show such fawning deference that the leader seems no longer merely human. Worse yet, sometimes the leader comes to enjoy his pedestal.

Paul faced this problem at Corinth. Christians there were splintering into camps promoting their favorite: some liked Apollos, others liked Paul. The apostle saw the danger and immediately put a stop to it. Neither of them warranted such favoritism, "but only God" (1 Cor. 3:7). Any fervor, devotion, or loyalty the people in Corinth might have for spiritual leaders should be fastened tightly to the person of Jesus.

Spiritual leaders may be "esteemed highly in love for their work's sake," but that esteem cannot degenerate into adulation. Leaders must work to attach the people's affection to Jesus. There is no fault in finding encouragement when one's service is appreciated, but the leader must altogether refuse to be idolized.

Stephen Neill said in a lecture to theological students: "Popularity is the most dangerous spiritual state imaginable, since it leads on so easily to the spiritual pride which drowns men in perdition. It is a symptom to be watched with anxiety since so often it has been purchased at the too heavy price of compromise with the world."[2]

Spurgeon also felt the danger of popularity pressing close to his heart:

> Success exposes a man to the pressure of people and thus tempts
> him to hold on to his gains by means of fleshly methods and
> practices, and to let himself be ruled wholly by the dictatorial
> demands of incessant expansion. Success can go to my head, and
> will unless I remember that it is God who accomplished the work,
> that He can continue to do so without any help, and that He will
> be able to make out with other means whenever He cuts me
> down to size.[3]

George Whitefield was immensely popular, and in his early years he enjoyed the acclaim. He recalled that he felt it was death to be despised and worse than death to be laughed at. But as his service and career progressed, he grew tired of the attention. "I have seen enough of popularity to be sick of it," he declared.

Infallibility

Spirituality does not guarantee infallible judgment. The Spirit-filled person is less likely to make mistakes of judgment than his secular counterpart; but perfection eludes us all, whatever our level of spiritual development. Even the apostles made mistakes that required divine correction.

Spiritual leaders who have given such a significant share of their lives to knowing God, to prayer, and to wrestling with the problems of renewal and revival may find it difficult to concede the possibility of misjudgment or mistake. Surely the leader must be a person of strength and decisiveness, to stand for what he believes. But willingness to concede error and to defer to the judgment of one's peers increases one's influence rather than diminishes it. Followers will lose confidence in a leader who appears to believe himself to be infallible. It is strange but true that a perception of infallibility in one area of life often coexists with great humility in other areas.

Indispensability

Many influential Christians have fallen before this temptation. It seems that Christians are especially prone to it. They cling to authority long after it should have passed to younger people. The author met a wonderful Christian in his nineties who was still superintendent of his church's Sunday School. Younger people were willing and available, but no one in the church had been able to approach this saint about retirement. One unfortunate consequence is that young people who have energy to fill a role are held up and stagnate.

Sometimes sincere and well-meaning followers encourage the notion of indispensability, which feeds a leader's ego and makes him even less objective about performance in office. And we do become less objective about our work as we get older.

The missionary who has raised a church to believe that he is indispensable has done the church an injustice. From the earliest days of the work, the missionary should be planning on working out of a job. National leadership needs to learn how to depend on the Lord, how to train its own spiritual leaders, and how to take responsibility for the work.

Elation and Depression

Every work of God includes days of frustration and days of joy. The leader is in peril of becoming overly depressed by the one and overly elated by the other. Discovering the balance here is not easy.

When the 70 disciples returned from their mission elated with results, Jesus checked their euphoria. "Do not rejoice that the spirits submit to you, but rejoice that your names are written in heaven" (Luke 10:20).

After the drama at Carmel, Elijah was so depressed that he wanted to die. The Lord corrected his self-pity in a most prosaic manner, by insisting on two long sleeps and two decent meals. Only then did the spiritual lessons begin, and they made a lifelong difference to Elijah. His discouragement was unfounded: seven thousand faithful Israelites had not yet bowed to Baal. By running away, Elijah had deprived this remnant of leadership they desperately needed.

Not all our ideals and goals for the work of God will be realized. People we trust will disappoint us; cherished plans will fall victim to shortfalls or sickness; the sacrifices leaders make will be interpreted as selfish gestures. Bad things happen, but the spiritual leader should discern the reasons for depression and deal with it accordingly.

F. B. Meyer was an eternal optimist, ever hopeful, ever vigorous, ever confident of the triumph of good over evil. But he was also far too keen and thoughtful a man. . . not to be overcome now and again by the pessimistic views of life. He occasionally went down into the very depths of human despair. He had seen too often and too clearly the seamy side of life not to be sad and pessimistic now and then.[4]

Another kind of depression is described by Spurgeon in his lecture, "The Minister's Fainting Fits":

> Before any great achievement, some measure of depression is very usual. . . . Such was my experience when I first became a pastor in London. My success appalled me, and the thought of the career which seemed to open up so far from elating me, cast me into the lowest depth, out of which I muttered my *miserere* and found no room for a *gloria in excelsis*. Who was I that I should continue to lead so great a multitude? I would betake me to my village obscurity, or emigrate to America and find a solitary nest in the backwoods where I might be sufficient for the things that were demanded of me. It was just then the curtain was rising on my lifework, and I dreaded what it might reveal. I hope I was not faithless, but I was timorous and filled with a sense of my own unfitness. . . . This depression comes over me whenever the Lord is preparing a larger blessing for my ministry.[5]

Seasons there are when all goes well. Goals are reached, plans find success, the Spirit moves, souls are saved, and saints blessed. When Robert Murray McCheyne went through times like this, he would kneel down and symbolically place the crown of success on the brow of the Lord, to whom it rightly belonged. That habit helped save him from assuming the glory for achievement that belonged to God alone.

Samuel Chadwick wisely said: "If successful, don't crow; if defeated, don't croak."[6]

Match the definition of the peril on the left with the description of the peril on the right.

1. Pride	_____ Greatly enjoying the attentions and adulation of people
2. Egotism	_____ Being suspicious of rivals
3. Popularity	_____ Taking personal credit for the abilities, positions, and gifts God has given
4. Jealousy	_____ Focusing on self-thinking and speaking always of one's attainments and achievements
5. Infallibility	_____ Overreacting to days of frustration or joy
6. Indispensability	_____ An unwillingness to concede error or defer to the judgment of others
7. Elation/depression	_____ Not willing to give up authority to others

**Circle any of the perils which cause you concern
right now in your life.**

Prophet or Leader?

Sometimes we come to a fork in the path, and both ways look good and true. For example, a preacher with gifts of leadership faces a decision whether to be a popular leader or an unpopular prophet. A. C. Dixon faced such a dilemma:

> Every preacher ought to be primarily a prophet of God who preaches as God bids him, without regard to results. When he becomes conscious of the fact that he is a leader in his own church or denomination, he has reached a crisis in his ministry. He must now choose one of two courses, that of prophet of God or a leader of men. If he seeks to be a prophet and a leader, he is apt to make a failure of both. If he decides to be a prophet only insofar as he can do without losing his leadership, he becomes a diplomat and ceases to be a prophet at all. If he decides to maintain leadership at all costs, he may easily fall to the level of a politician who pulls the wires in order to gain or hold a position.[7]

Dixon maximizes the differences between leader and prophet; in reality, however, the roles overlap. But situations develop in which a leader must choose between a spiritual ministry and a leadership that would prevent the highest exercise of that ministry. Herein lies the peril.

Reuben A. Torrey, whom God used at the turn of the century to bring revival to half the world, faced such a choice. Dixon wrote of him:

> The thousands who have heard Dr. Torrey know the man and his message. He loves the Bible, and believing it to be the infallible Word of God, preaches it with the fervor of red-hot conviction. He never compromises. He has chosen to be a prophet of God rather than a mere leader of men, and that is the secret of his power with God and men.[8]

Disqualification

Despite his success as a missionary and leader, Paul was never without a wholesome, watchful fear that after having preached to others, he himself might be disqualified (1 Cor. 9:27). To him this prospect was an ever-present warning against smugness and complacency. So should it be to all who are entrusted with spiritual responsibility.

The Greek word for "disqualified" (in other translations "castaway" or "disapproved") in verse 27 is used of metals that were not suitable for coinage. Those metals could not survive the test; the refining process had left them below standard. Paul refers here to losing the coveted prize for failure to comply with the rules of the contest.

Paul's metaphor puts him in two roles here. He is a competitor in the contest, and also the herald who announces the rules of the game and calls runners to the starting line. Paul feared that after acting as a herald (preaching), he himself should fail by the very standards he preached. In that case, his position as herald would only serve to aggravate his own guilt, shame, and disgrace.

The failure before Paul's eyes here is failure of the body, and to guard against it requires rigorous self-discipline. Charles Hodge affirms that in Scripture the body is "the seat and organ of sin, [and refers to] our whole sinful nature. It was not merely his sensual nature Paul endeavored to bring into subjection, but all the evil propensities of his heart."[9]

Paul believed he could be disqualified not merely because of errors of doctrine or misjudgments of ethics, but because of the body's passions. Paul worked toward mastering the body's appetites through disciplined moderation—neither asceticism on the one hand (such as causing oneself harm by denial of basic needs) or self-indulgence on the other (losing strength through careless diet, for example). Paul was not willing to give in to bodily appetites, as if they were his master. He insisted on being in command of his own bodily needs and wants. A. S. Way rendered this passage: "I browbeat my own animal nature, and treat it not as my master but my slave."

---

[1] Robert Louis Stevenson, in *The Reaper*, July 1942, 96.

[2] Stephen Neill, in *The Record*, 28 March 1947, 161.

[3] Helmut Thielecke, *Encounter with Spurgeon* (Philadelphia: Fortress, 1963).

[4] W. Y. Fullerton, *F. B. Meyer* (London: Marshall, Morgan & Scott, n.d.), 172.

[5] Quoted in Thielecke, 219.

[6] N. G. Dunning, *Samuel Chadwick* (London: Hodder & Stoughton, 1934), 206.

[7] H. C. A. Dixon, *A. C. Dixon* (New York: Putnam, 1931), 277. Amzi Clarence Dixon (1854–1925) served as pastor of Moody Memorial Church and the Metropolitan Tabernacle of London.

[8] Ibid., 158. Reuben Archer Torrey (1856–1928), a Congregationalist minister, was first superintendent of the Moody Bible Institute (then called Chicago Evangelization Society) and pastor of Moody Memorial Church (then Chicago Avenue Church). He conducted crusades in Europe, Asia, and the Orient. He was later president of the Bible Institute of Los Angeles (now Biola University) and pastor of Church of the Open Door in downtown Los Angeles.

[9] Charles Hodge (1797–1878), quoted here without citation, was professor of theology at Princeton Seminary. A conservative Presbyterian on matters of doctrine, he also believed that the Bible permitted slavery and condemned only its abuse, a position which caused him immense controversy during the peak of his career.

The Leader Nehemiah

Remember me with favor, O my God.
—Nehemiah 13:31

Nehemiah is one of the most inspiring leaders in the Bible. At times his methods seem somewhat vigorous, but they were used by God to achieve spectacular reforms in the life of his nation in an amazingly short time. An analysis of his personality and methods discloses that the methods he adopted were effective only because of the quality of his own character.

His Character

The first impression a reader gains from this straightforward story is that Nehemiah was a man of prayer. For Nehemiah, prayer was an ordinary part of living and working. Prayer was his first reaction on hearing the plight of emigrants in Jerusalem. Nehemiah was no stranger at the throne of grace (Neh. 1:4, 6; 2:4; 4:4, 9; 5:19; 6:14; 13:14, 22, 29).

He showed courage in the face of danger. "Should a man like me run away? Or should one like me go into the temple to save his life? I will not go!" (6:11). Such firm fearlessness would inspire any discouraged people.

His genuine concern for the welfare of others was so obvious that even his enemies noticed it (2:10). He expressed his concern in fasting, prayer, and tears (1:4-6). Nehemiah identified with his people in their sorrows and in their sins: "I confess the sins we Israelites, including myself and my father's house, have committed against you" (1:6).

Nehemiah exhibited keen foresight. He knew that opposition was sure to arise; so he secured letters from the king for safe passage and for the resources to accomplish the task, "to make beams for the gates of the citadel . . . and for the city wall" (2:8). He carefully planned his strategy.

Through all his adventures and boldness, there runs a strain of caution. He did not jump into the work immediately upon arrival, but waited three days to appraise the situation (2:11). And when he did set to business, he did not hold a tell-all press conference, but kept his goals largely secret, even doing reconnaissance under cover of night.

Nehemiah could make clear decisions. He did not put off the tough call, but cut to the heart and made a judgment. And his decisions were impartial; he did not play favorites. When censure was needed, he gave it to officials and executives as well as to workers (5:7).

Nehemiah was uncommonly empathetic. He listened to grievances and took remedial action (4:10-14; 5:1-13). He let people "weep on his shoulder." He sympathized with others.

Nehemiah was a realist; he understood the mechanics of the real world. "We prayed to our God and posted a guard day and night" (4:9).

He accepted responsibility with the intention of following through on all assignments, the pleasant ones and the dirty ones, until the job was done.

Nehemiah was a vigorous administrator, a calm crisis manager, a fearless initiator, a courageous decision maker, and a persevering leader. He was resolute in the face of threats and vigilant against treachery—a leader who won and held the full confidence of his followers.

> **Scan pages 134-135 and underline all of the character descriptions of Nehemiah.**
>
> **Put a star by those descriptions which you would like to develop in your life as a leader.**

His Methods

Nehemiah raised the morale of his colleagues, an important part of any leader's work. He built up their faith by redirecting focus away from "the impossible" toward the greatness of God. Throughout the record are such assurances as "the God of heaven will give us success" (2:20) and "the joy of the LORD is your strength" (8:10).

> **How do the people benefit when the leader directs the focus away from "the impossible" and toward the greatness of God?**

Faith builds faith. Pessimism dismantles faith. The spiritual leader's primary task is to build the faith of others.

Nehemiah encouraged others generously. When he arrived, the people were discouraged and demoralized. First he kindled hope by testifying to the vision and providence of God, and then he secured their cooperation. "I also told them about the gracious hand of my God upon me and what the king had said to me. They replied, 'Let us start building.' So they began this good work" (2:18).

Faults and failures must be corrected, but method makes all the difference. Nehemiah could point to people's shortcomings and find hope for a better day. Then his faith and great personal discipline won their confidence and established his authority.

Identify a problem you are facing in your ministry.

How can you follow the example of Nehemiah in dealing with this problem?

Nehemiah promptly faced potential weaknesses in the plan. Two cases illustrate.

The people were discouraged and tired. Opponents were making life miserable (4:10-18). Garbage was piling up and hampering progress. Nehemiah first directed their vision to God, then put them under arms and deployed them at strategic points. He harnessed the strength of the family unit, ordering half a family to work while the other half stood guard and rested. The people recovered their courage as Nehemiah solved real problems through decisive action.

What actions can you take to prepare yourself to deal with the opposition?

In the second instance the people were disillusioned by the greed of their own rich brothers (5:1-15). Most people lived on mortgaged land; some had sold children as slaves to meet expenses. "Neither is it in our power to redeem them; for other men have our lands and vineyards" (v. 5, KJV). What an awkward mess: children of "have nots" victims of an economy where wealth was held in the hands of a few, and those few were not about to release their grasp.

Nehemiah listened to their stories and sympathized with their suffering. He rebuked the nobles for their heartless usury (5:7) and appealed for immediate relief (v. 11). So effective was his negotiation that the reply of the nobles was simply, "We will do as you say" (v. 12).

Nehemiah recovered the authority of the Word of God in the lives of the people (8:1-8). The reforms he instituted would have been short-lived or even impossible apart from that. He restored the Feast of Tabernacles, which had not been observed since Joshua's day. He led the people to repentance through the reading of the law (9:3-5). He purified the temple of pagan influence (13:4-9). He encouraged tithing, established Sabbath rest, forbade intermarriage with pagan foreigners, and so recovered the special identity of Israel as God's chosen people.

Nehemiah could organize projects and people. Before making detailed plans he conducted a careful survey of the situation (2:11-16). He made a detailed assessment of the personnel available. He did not neglect unglamorous paperwork. He then established key objectives, assigned those to responsible leaders (men of faith and piety), and set them to work (7:1-3). He gave adequate recognition to subordinate leaders, mentioning them by name and the place where each worked (3:1-32). They were given a sense that they were more than mere cogs in a machine. He practiced a wise delegation of responsibility. "I put in charge of Jerusalem my brother Hanani, along with Hananiah the commander of the citadel" (7:2a). He had high standards for the subordinates whom he chose, selecting Hananiah, for example, "because he was a man of integrity and feared God more than most men do" (7:2b). All of this opened the leadership potential of others.

In the above paragraph underline Nehemiah's organizational skills.

Nehemiah faced up to opposition without forcing a violent confrontation. He took insults, innuendo, intimidation, and treachery. He walked through it with his head high and his eyes wide open, with much prayer (4:9). When he could, he simply ignored the adversary. Always he took precautions (v. 16). Never did he allow opposition to deflect his energy from the central task. Always he kept faith in God (v. 20).

The test of spiritual leadership is the achievement of its objective. In Nehemiah's case, the record is clear: "So the wall was completed" (6:15).

As you review Nehemiah's leadership qualities, which ones would you like to develop in your life?

Leadership Check-up

You are encouraged to spend time with God, reviewing the concepts you have studied in this book and identifying any changes you are going to make under the guidance of the Holy Spirit.

1. What is your greatest leadership challenge?

2. Have you committed this to the Lord?

3. What do you sense God would have you do next in developing your leadership skills?

4. Do you sense any specific person(s) whom God has called you to mentor?

5. What specific action(s) will you begin with this person(s)?

Group Study Questions

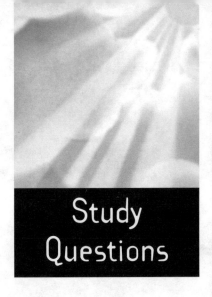

Spiritual Leadership is a helpful book for almost everyone who wants to improve his or her leadership abilities. But, study and discussion of the book with a small group of close friends can bring even greater benefit. This study guide was developed to allow small groups to discuss the concepts in the book in six sessions. The format for each session is divided into three parts.

Get Started begins with common life experiences and helps all group members get involved in the discussion. For a one-hour session, spend no more than five minutes on these questions.

Get the Point focuses on the main point of three or four chapters in the book and provides further discussion on key Bible passages. These questions will typically require 40–45 minutes of discussion time.

Get Going moves group members into the action phase with suggestions for life application. Reserve about 10–15 minutes to discuss these questions.

Have each group member read the assigned chapters and complete the chapters' interactive questions. Because many of the interactive questions are personal, make sure the participants know that the group discussions will be based on the group study questions. Be sure to open and close your discussion with prayer.

STUDY 1

Read chapters 1–3 in *Spiritual Leadership,* then prepare answers to the following questions for group discussion.

Get Started

1. Tell about a time you aspired to be a leader in some area of life. What position did you aspire to? What happened?

Get the Point

2. Why is it difficult for Christians today to agree wholeheartedly with Paul that spiritual leadership is "an honorable ambition"? (chap. 1)

3. Why are spiritual leaders in such short supply today? (chap. 2)

4. What is the role of leadership training if spiritual leadership is conferred by God alone? (chap. 2)

5. How do the leadership qualities admired in the business world compare to the qualities required for spiritual leaders? (Mark 10:41-45)

6. How would you describe "servant leadership" to a young, successful entrepreneur who recently became a Christian? (chap. 3)

7. How would your church be different if it developed the spiritual leadership described in this chapter? (chap. 3)

8. What is the most significant insight about spiritual leadership that you have gained by reading these first three chapters?

Get Going

9. What ambitions for leadership do you need to restrain?

10. Where do you most need to exhibit an attitude of selfless service?

STUDY 2

Read chapters 4–7 in *Spiritual Leadership*, then prepare answers to the following questions for group discussion.

Get Started

1. What "natural" leadership qualities do others say you possess?

Get the Point

2. In your opinion, what is the key difference between natural leadership and spiritual leadership? (chap. 4)

Presence of God
self serving   God-serving

3. How is natural leadership transformed into spiritual leadership? (chap. 4)

obedience   Brokenness

4. Which of the items in Sanders's list concern you the most in your own development as a leader? (chap. 5)

5. How does your church decide when someone is fit for spiritual leadership? How is the process working? (chap. 6)

6. What advice from Paul about leadership is timely for you? (chap. 6)

7. What deficiencies and failings do you most often notice in leaders? (chap. 7)

8. Is it important for someone to fail as badly as Peter did, in order to have a humble heart? How have people you know learned humility? (chap. 7)

9. Who do you prefer as a model of leadership, Peter or Paul? Why?

Get Going

10. What one quality of spiritual leadership needs the most attention in your life? How can you get started on it this week?

STUDY 3

Read chapters 8–10 in *Spiritual Leadership*, then prepare answers to the following questions for group discussion.

Get Started

1. If you were granted a wish and could instantly and permanently acquire one leadership quality, which would you select?

Get the Point

2. How can vision create problems? (chap. 8)

3. Can serious people learn to be funny?
   Why is it difficult to maintain a sense of humor when leading? (chap. 9)

4. How can anger help a leader? How can it hurt? (chap. 9)

5. Why is patience a particularly difficult virtue for leaders to develop? (chap. 9)

6. What leadership qualities do you think are in shortest supply among Christians?

7. When faced with a decision to do something or go somewhere, how can a leader tell the difference between promptings from the Holy Spirit and inclinations of the self? (chap. 10)

8. What is the difference between being naturally gifted in leadership and being spiritually gifted? (chap. 10)

Get Going

9. Give yourself a report card on your leadership qualities. Where have you made improvement recently? Where do you still need some more work?

STUDY 4

Read chapters 11–14 in *Spiritual Leadership*, then prepare answers to the following questions for group discussion.

Get Started

1. During an average week, to which of these activities do you give the most time: lawn care/house projects? book/magazine/newspaper reading? television/movie viewing? prayer?

Get the Point

2. When have you felt sorrowful about your prayer life? What changes did you make? (chap. 11)

3. What are some of the obstacles that keep people from prayer? (chap. 11)

4. If time were not a consideration, what work in the church would you most enjoy? (chap. 12)

5. Why do spiritual leaders often feel undue pressure in the use of time? (chap. 12)

6. If you were stranded on an island, what three books (or magazine subscriptions) would you most desire? (chap. 13)

7. If the notes and files of your reading were to be turned over to a detective-psychologist for character analysis, what would he or she conclude about you? (chap. 13)

8. What does it mean to lead with intensity?
   How does a person learn to do this? (chap. 14)

9. Discuss the idea that spiritual leadership is always top down, not bottom up. What extremes pose dangers for this view? What problems does this view solve? (chap. 14)

Get Going

10. What step could you take this week to start making better use of your time for God's kingdom?

11. How can you find the time you need for prayer?

STUDY 5

Read chapters 15–18 in *Spiritual Leadership*, then prepare answers to the following questions for group discussion.

Get Started

1. Leadership can be difficult and demanding. What price are you willing to pay?

Get the Point

2. What does it mean for a leader to take up his or her cross? (chap. 15)

3. How should leaders handle just criticism and rejection? (chap. 15)

4. Which of Benson's rules for living is most difficult for you to follow? (chap. 16)

5. What's the difference between good compromise (the opposite of stubbornness) and bad compromise (the opposite of commitment)? How can you tell when compromise is right and good? (chap. 17)

6. How long does it take you to overcome the feeling of failure? With whom do you discuss failure? (chap. 17)

7. Which test of leadership do you fear the most? (chap. 17)

8. How do you know that you have communicated instructions carefully enough? How can your ambiguities in delegation return to haunt you? (chap. 18)

9. What do you do, or where do you go, for renewal from fatigue?

Get Going

10. What steps can you take this week to better prepare you for the tests of leadership you may eventually face in the future?

STUDY SIX

Read chapters 19–22 in *Spiritual Leadership*, then prepare answers to the following questions for group discussion.

Get Started

1. What changes have been difficult for you in the past year? At work? At church? At home?

Get the Point

2. Looking back, how has God been at work preparing you for leadership? (chap. 19)

3. From what have you "retired" because your best contribution was over or the time was ripe for another leader? What were your feelings? (chap. 19)

4. Popularity holds what dangers for a leader? (chap. 20)

5. Which of the perils of leadership worry you the most? (chap. 21)

6. What areas of "moderation" are crucial to your fitness for spiritual service? (chap. 21)

7. How do you deal with people who believe they are never wrong? (chap. 21)

8. What do you most admire about Nehemiah's leadership? (chap. 22)

9. When you look ahead to the end of your life, what "walls" do you want to see standing? (chap. 22)

10. To what degree should men and women aspire to different leadership roles?

Get Going

11. How can you direct your own energies to do better the work God has for you?

Index of Scripture

Index of Scripture

Index of Scripture

Index of Scripture

Index of Persons

Index of Persons

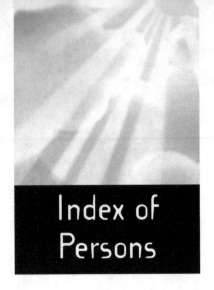

Index of Persons

Index of Persons